WHAT EVERY

BODY

IS SAYING

ALSO BY JOE NAVARRO WITH MARVIN KARLINS

Phil Hellmuth Presents Read 'Em and Reap

wm
WILLIAM MORROW
An Imprint of HarperCollins*Publishers*

WHAT EVERY
BODY
IS SAYING

An Ex-FBI Agent's Guide
to Speed-Reading People

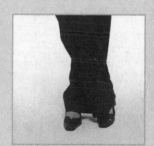

JOE NAVARRO
FBI Special Agent (Ret.)

with Marvin Karlins, Ph.D.

HarperCollins books may be purchased for educational, business, or sales promotional use. For information, please e-mail the Special Markets Department at SPsales@harpercollins.com.

FIRST EDITION

While the manuscript for this book was reviewed by the Federal Bureau of Investigation prior to publication, the opinions and thoughts expressed herein are those of the author exclusively.

Designed by Susan Walsh
Photographs by Mark Wemple
Illustrations (except for the limbic brain diagram) by David R. Andrade

Library of Congress Cataloging-in-Publication Data
   Navarro, Joe, 1953–
      What every BODY is saying : an ex-FBI agent's guide to speed-reading people / by Joe Navarro, with Marvin Karlins. – 1st ed.
         p. cm.
      Includes bibliographical references and index.
      ISBN 978-0-06-143829-5
      1. Body language.   2. Noverbal commbuication.   I. Karlins, Marvin.   II. Title.
      BF637.N66N38 2008
      153.6'9—dc22   2007042615

               17   40 39 38 37 36 35 34 33 32 31

To my grandmother, Adelina, whose withered
hands lovingly molded a child into a man.
—JOE NAVARRO

To my wife, Edyth, who has blessed me with her love
and taught me what it means to be a caring human being.
—MARVIN KARLINS

CONTENTS

FOREWORD

I See What You're Thinking

Marvin Karlins, Ph.D.

The man sat stoically at one end of the table, carefully crafting his replies to the FBI agent's inquiries. He wasn't considered a major suspect in the murder case. His alibi was believable and he sounded sincere, but the agent pressed on nevertheless. With the suspect's consent, he was asked a series of questions about the murder weapon:

> "If you had committed this crime, would you have used a gun?"
> "If you had committed this crime, would you have used a knife?"
> "If you had committed this crime, would you have used an ice pick?"
> "If you had committed this crime, would you have used a hammer?"

One of the weapons, the ice pick, had actually been used in the commission of the crime, but that information had been kept from the public. Thus, only the killer would know which object was the real murder weapon. As the FBI agent went down the list of weapons, he observed the suspect carefully. When the ice pick was mentioned, the man's eyelids came down hard and stayed down until the next weapon was named. The agent instantly understood the significance of the eyelid behavior he had witnessed, and from that moment forward the "minor" suspect became the primary person of interest in the investigation. He later confessed to the crime.

Chalk one up for Joe Navarro, a remarkable human being who, in addition to unmasking the ice-pick killer, is credited with catching scores of criminals, including "master spies," in a distinguished twenty-five-year career with the FBI. How was he able to do this? If you asked him, he quietly would say, "I owe it to being able to read people."

Joe, it turns out, has spent his entire professional life studying, refining, and applying the science of nonverbal communications—facial expressions, gestures, physical movements (kinesics), body distance (proxemics), touching (haptics), posture, even clothing—to decipher what people are thinking, how they intend to act, and whether their pronouncements are true or false. This is *not* good news for criminals, terrorists, and spies, who, under his careful scrutiny, usually give off more than enough nonverbal body signals ("tells") to make their thoughts and intentions transparent and detectable.

It is, however, very good news for you, the reader, because the very same nonverbal knowledge Joe relied on to become a master "Spycatcher," "human lie detector," and instructor at the FBI is what he will be sharing with you so you can better understand the feelings, thoughts, and intentions of those around you. As a renowned author and educator, Joe will teach you how to observe like an expert, detecting and deciphering the nonverbal behaviors of others so you can interact with them more successfully. For business or for pleasure, this knowledge will enrich and magnify your life.

Much of what Joe will be sharing with you in this book was not even recognized fifteen years ago by the scientific community. It is only through recent advances in brain-scan technology and neural imaging that scientists have been able to establish the validity of the behaviors Joe will be describing. Drawing from the latest discoveries in psychology, neurobiology, medicine, sociology, criminology, communication studies, and anthropology—plus his quarter century of experience using non-verbal behavior in his work as an FBI Special Agent—Joe is uniquely qualified to help you succeed in your understanding of nonverbal com-munications. His expertise is recognized and sought worldwide. Besides being interviewed regularly on programs such as NBC's *Today Show, CNN Headline News, Fox Cable News,* and ABC's *Good Morning America*, he continues to conduct seminars on nonverbal communication for the FBI and the CIA, as well as for other members of the intelligence com-munity. He is a consultant to the banking and insurance industries as well as to major law firms in the United States and abroad. Joe also teaches at Saint Leo University and at various medical schools through-out the United States, where his unique insights into nonverbal com-munication have found a receptive audience among many, including physicians desiring to assess patients with greater speed and accuracy. Joe's combination of academic skills and occupational credentials—coupled with his masterful analysis of nonverbal communications in real-life, high-stakes situations—has placed him apart and in the forefront of nonverbal expertise, as you will discover in this book.

After working with Joe, attending his seminars, and putting his ideas to work in my own life, I firmly believe that the material in these pages represents a major advance in our understanding of all things nonverbal. I say this as a trained psychologist who got involved in this writing proj-ect because I was excited by Joe's pioneering work in harnessing the *sci-entific* knowledge of nonverbal communications to achieve professional objectives and personal success.

I was also impressed by his reasoned, careful approach to the topic. For example, while observing nonverbals allows us to get an "accurate read" on many kinds of behavior, Joe warns us that using body language to detect deception is a particularly difficult and challenging task. This is a significant insight—rarely recognized by laypeople or by the law en-forcement community—and serves as a critical and poignant reminder to be *very* careful before you declare a person to be honest or dishonest based on his nonverbal behaviors.

Unlike many other books on nonverbal behavior, the information presented herein is based on scientific facts and field-tested findings rather than on personal opinion and armchair speculations. Further, the text highlights what other published works often ignore: the critical role played by the *limbic system* of the human brain in understanding and using nonverbal cues effectively.

The silent language of the body can be yours to master. Whether you are studying nonverbals because you want to get ahead in your job or simply want to get along better with friends and family, this book is designed for you. Gaining proficiency will require a careful examination of the chapters that follow, plus a commitment to spend some serious time and energy learning and applying Joe's teachings in your daily routines.

Reading people successfully—learning, decoding, and utilizing nonverbal behavior to predict human actions—is a task well worth your attention, one that offers ample rewards for the effort expended. So plant your feet firmly on the floor, turn to the next page, and get ready to learn and watch for those all-important nonverbal behaviors that Joe will be teaching you. It won't be long before you discover, with just a glance, what every *body* is saying.

ACKNOWLEDGMENTS

When I started writing the early drafts of this book, I realized that this project had been long in the making. It did not start with my interest in reading about nonverbal behavior, nor in pursuing it academically, nor in the FBI. Rather, in a real sense, it started with my family many years earlier.

I learned to read others primarily from the teachings of my parents, Albert and Mariana Lopez, and my grandmother, Adelina Paniagua Espino. Each in his or her own way taught me something different about the significance and power of nonverbal communications. From my mother, I learned that nonverbals are invaluable in dealing with others. A subtle behavior, she taught me, can avert an awkward situation or can make someone completely comfortable—a skill she has performed effortlessly all of her life. From my father, I learned the power of expression;

with one look he can communicate volumes with exquisite clarity. He is a man who commands respect, just by being. And from my grandmother, to whom I dedicate this book, I learned that small behaviors have great significance: a smile, a head tilt, a gentle touch at the right time can convey so much; it can even heal. These things they taught me every day, and in so doing, prepared me to observe more aptly the world around me. Their teachings as well as those of many others are found in these pages.

While I was at Brigham Young University, J. Wesley Sherwood, Richard Townsend, and Dean Clive Winn II taught me much about police work and observing criminals. Later, in the FBI, people such as Doug Gregory, Tom Riley, Julian "Jay" Koerner, Dr. Richard Ault, and David G. Major taught me the subtle nuances of counterintelligence and espionage behavior. To them I am grateful for sharpening my people-watching skills. Similarly, I have to thank Dr. John Schafer, former FBI agent and fellow member of the bureau's elite Behavioral Analysis Program, who encouraged me to write and allowed me to be his coauthor on multiple occasions. Marc Reeser, who was with me in the trenches catching spies for so long, also deserves my recognition. To my other colleagues, and there were many in the National Security Division of the FBI, I thank you for all your support.

Over the years, the FBI ensured we were taught by the best, and so at the hands of professors Joe Kulis, Paul Ekman, Maureen O'Sullivan, Mark Frank, Bella M. DePaulo, Aldert Vrij, Reid Meloy, and Judy Burgoon I learned about the research on nonverbal communications directly or through their writings. I developed a friendship with many of these individuals, including David Givens, who heads the Center for Nonverbal Studies in Spokane, Washington, and whose writings, teachings, and admonitions I have taken to heart. Their research and writings have enriched my life, and I have included their work in this volume as well as that of other giants such as Desmond Morris, Edward Hall, and Charles Darwin, who started it all with his seminal book *The expression of the emotions in man and animals.*

While these people provided the academic framework, others contributed in their own ways to this project, and I must recognize them individually. My dear friend Elizabeth Lee Barron, at the University of Tampa, is a godsend when it comes to research. I am also indebted to Dr. Phil Quinn at the University of Tampa and to Professor Barry Glover, at Saint Leo University, for their years of friendship and willingness to accommodate my busy travel schedule.

This book would not be the same without photographs, and for that I am grateful for the work of renowned photographer Mark Wemple. My gratitude also goes out to Ashlee B. Castle, my administrative assistant, who, when asked if she was willing to make faces for a book, merely said, "Sure, why not?" You guys are great. I also want to thank Tampa artist David R. Andrade for his illustrations.

Matthew Benjamin, my ever-patient editor at HarperCollins, put this project together and deserves my praise for being a gentleman and a consummate professional. My praise also goes to Executive Editor Toni Sciarra, who worked so diligently to finalize this project. Matthew and Toni work with a wonderful team of people at HarperCollins, including copy editor Paula Cooper, to whom I owe many thanks. And as before, I want to thank Dr. Marvin Karlins for once again shaping my ideas into this book and for his kind words in the foreword.

My gratitude goes out to my dear friend Dr. Elizabeth A. Murray, a true scientist and educator, who took time out from her busy teaching schedule to edit the early drafts of this manuscript and share her voluminous knowledge of the human body.

To my family—all of my family, near and far—I thank you for tolerating me and my writing when I should have been relaxing with you. To Luca, *muito obrigado*. To my daughter, Stephanie, I give thanks every day for your loving soul.

All of these individuals have contributed to this book in some way; their knowledge and insight, small and large, is shared with you herein. I wrote this book with the sober knowledge that many of you will use this information in your daily lives. To that end, I have worked assiduously to present both the science and the empirical information with diligence and clarity. If there are any errors in this book, they are my responsibility and mine alone.

There is an old Latin saying, "Qui docet, discit" (He who teaches, learns). In many ways, writing is no different; it is a process of learning and discerning, which at the end of the day has been a pleasure. It is my hope that when you come to the end of this book, you too will have gained a profound knowledge of how we communicate nonverbally— and that your life will be enriched, as mine has been, by knowing what every *body* is saying.

Joe Navarro
Tampa, Florida
August 2007

WHAT EVERY
BODY
IS SAYING

ONE

Mastering the Secrets of Nonverbal Communication

Whenever I'm teaching people about "body language," this question is invariably asked. "Joe, what got you interested in studying nonverbal behavior in the first place?" It wasn't something I had planned to do, nor was it the result of some long-term fascination with the topic. It was much more down-to-earth than that. It was an interest born of necessity, the need to adapt successfully to a totally new way of life. When I was eight years old, I came to America as an exile from Cuba. We left just a few months after the Bay of Pigs invasion, and we honestly thought we would be here only for a short while as refugees.

Unable to speak English at first, I did what thousands of other immigrants coming to this country have done. I quickly learned that to fit in with my new classmates at school, I needed to be aware of—and sensitive to—the "other" language around me, the language of nonverbal behavior. I found that was a language I *could* translate and understand immediately. In my young mind, I saw the human body as a kind of billboard that transmitted (advertised) what a person was thinking via gestures, facial expressions, and physical movements that I could read. Over time, obviously, I learned English—and even lost some skill with the Spanish language—but the nonverbals, I never forgot. I discovered at an early age that I could always rely on nonverbal communications.

I learned to use body language to decipher what my classmates and teachers were trying to communicate to me and how they felt about me. One of the first things I noticed was that students or teachers who genuinely liked me would raise (or arch) their eyebrows when they first saw me walk into the room. On the other hand, those individuals who weren't too friendly toward me would squint their eyes slightly when I appeared—a behavior that once observed is never forgotten. I used this nonverbal information, as so many other immigrants have, quickly to evaluate and develop friendships, to communicate despite the obvious language barrier, to avoid enemies, and in nurturing healthy relationships. Many years later I would use these same nonverbal eye behaviors to solve crimes as a special agent at the Federal Bureau of Investigation (FBI) (see box 1).

Based on my background, education, and training, I want to teach you to see the world as an FBI expert on nonverbal communication views it: as a vivid, dynamic environment where every human interaction resonates with information, and as an opportunity to use the silent language of the body to enrich your knowledge of what people are thinking, feeling, and intending to do. Using this knowledge will help you stand out among others. It will also protect you and give you previously hidden insight into human behavior.

WHAT EXACTLY IS NONVERBAL COMMUNICATION?

Nonverbal communication, often referred to as nonverbal behavior or body language, is a means of transmitting information—just like the spoken word—except it is achieved through facial expressions, gestures,

BOX 1: **IN THE BLINK OF AN EYE**

"Eye-blocking" is a nonverbal behavior that can occur when we feel threatened and/or don't like what we see. Squinting (as in the case with my classmates, described above) and closing or shielding our eyes are actions that have evolved to protect the brain from "seeing" undesirable images and to communicate our disdain toward others.

As an investigator, I used eye-blocking behaviors to assist in the arson investigation of a tragic hotel fire in Puerto Rico that claimed ninety-seven lives. A security guard came under immediate suspicion because the blaze broke out in an area where he was assigned. One of the ways we determined he had nothing to do with starting the fire was by asking him some very specific questions as to where he was before the fire, at the time of the fire, and whether or not he set the fire. After each question I observed his face for any telltale signs of eye-block behavior. His eyes blocked only when questioned about where he was when the fire started. Oddly, in contrast, he did not seem troubled by the question, "Did you set the fire?" This told me the real issue was his location at the time of the fire, not his possible involvement in setting the fire. He was questioned further on this topic by the lead investigators and eventually admitted to leaving his post to visit his girlfriend, who also worked at the hotel. Unfortunately, while he was gone, the arsonists entered the area he should have been guarding and started the fire.

In this case, the guard's eye-blocking behavior gave us the insight we needed to pursue a line of questioning that eventually broke the case open. In the end, three arsonists responsible for the tragic blaze were arrested and convicted of the crime. The security guard, while woefully negligent and burdened with tremendous guilt, was not, however, the culprit.

touching (haptics), physical movements (kinesics), posture, body adornment (clothes, jewelry, hairstyle, tattoos, etc.), and even the tone, timbre,
and volume of an individual's voice (rather than spoken content).
Nonverbal behaviors comprise approximately 60 to 65 percent of all
interpersonal communication and, during lovemaking, can constitute
100 percent of communication between partners (Burgoon, 1994,
229–285).

Nonverbal communication can also reveal a person's true thoughts,
feelings, and intentions. For this reason, nonverbal behaviors are sometimes referred to as *tells* (they tell us about the person's true state of
mind). Because people are not always aware they are communicating
nonverbally, body language is often more honest than an individual's
verbal pronouncements, which are consciously crafted to accomplish the
speaker's objectives (see box 2).

BOX 2: **ACTIONS SPEAK LOUDER THAN WORDS**

A memorable example of how body language can sometimes be more
truthful than verbal language involved the rape of a young woman on the
Parker Indian Reservation in Arizona. A suspect in the case was brought
in for questioning. His words sounded convincing and his story was plausible. He claimed he hadn't seen the victim and while out in a field had
gone down a row of cotton, turned left, and then walked straight to his
house. While my colleagues jotted down notes about what they were
hearing, I kept my eyes on the suspect and saw that as he told the story
about turning left and going home, his hand gestured *to his right*, which
was exactly the direction that led to the rape scene. If I hadn't been
watching him, I wouldn't have caught the discrepancy between his verbal
("I went left") and nonverbal (hand gesturing to the right) behavior. But
once I saw it I suspected he was lying. I waited a while and then confronted him again, and in the end he confessed to the crime.

Whenever your observation of another person's nonverbal behavior helps you understand that person's feelings, intentions, or actions—or clarifies his or her spoken words—then you have successfully decoded and used this silent medium.

USING NONVERBAL BEHAVIOR TO
ENHANCE YOUR LIFE

It has been well established by researchers that those who can effectively read and interpret nonverbal communication, and manage how others perceive them, will enjoy greater success in life than individuals who lack this skill (Goleman, 1995, 13–92). It is the goal of this book to teach you how to observe the world around you and to determine the meaning of nonverbals in any setting. This powerful knowledge will enhance your personal interactions and enrich your life, as it has mine.

One of the fascinating things about an appreciation for nonverbal behavior is its universal applicability. It works everywhere humans interact. Nonverbals are ubiquitous and reliable. Once you know what a specific nonverbal behavior means, you can use that information in any number of different circumstances and in all types of environments. In fact, it is difficult to interact effectively without nonverbals. If you ever wondered why people still fly to meetings in the age of computers, text messages, e-mails, telephones, and video conferencing, it is because of the need to express and observe nonverbal communications in person. Nothing beats seeing the nonverbals up close and personal. Why? Because nonverbals are powerful and they have meaning. Whatever you learn from this book, you will be able to apply to any situation, in any setting. Case in point (see box 3 on next page):

Several months ago I presented a seminar to a group of poker players on how to use nonverbal behavior to read their opponents' hands and win more money at the tables. Because poker is a game that emphasizes bluffing and deception, players have a keen interest in being able to read the tells of their opponents. For them, decoding nonverbal communications is critical to success. While many were grateful for the insights I provided, what startled me was how many seminar participants were able to see the value of understanding and utilizing nonverbal behavior beyond the poker table.

Two weeks after the session ended I received an e-mail from one of the participants, a physician from Texas. "What I find most amazing," he wrote me, "is that what I learned in your seminar has also helped me in my practice. The nonverbals you taught us in order to read poker players have helped me read my patients, too. Now I can sense when they are uncomfortable, confident, or not being entirely truthful." The doctor's note speaks to the universality of nonverbals and their value in all facets of life.

MASTERING NONVERBAL COMMUNICATIONS REQUIRES A PARTNERSHIP

I am convinced that any person possessing normal intelligence can learn to use nonverbal communication to better themselves. I know this because for the past two decades I have taught thousands of people, just like you, how to successfully decode nonverbal behavior and use that information to enrich their lives, the lives of their loved ones, and to achieve their personal and professional goals. Accomplishing this, however, requires that you and I establish a working partnership, each contributing something of significance to our mutual effort.

Following the Ten Commandments for Observing and Decoding Nonverbal Communications Successfully

Reading people successfully—collecting nonverbal intelligence to assess their thoughts, feelings, and intentions—is a skill that requires constant practice and proper training. To help you on the training side, I want to provide you with some important guidelines—or commandments—to maximize your effectiveness in reading nonverbals. As you incorporate these commandments into your everyday life and make them part of your routine, they soon will become second nature to you, needing little, if any, conscious thought. It's a lot like learning to drive. Do you remember the first time you gave that a go? If you were like me, you were so concerned with operating the vehicle that it was difficult to track what you were doing *inside* the car and concentrate on what was happening on the road *outside* at the same time. It was only when you felt comfortable behind the wheel that you were able to expand your focus to encompass the total driving environment. That's the way it is with nonverbal behavior. Once you master the mechanics of using nonverbal communication effectively, it will become automatic and you can focus your full attention on decoding the world around you.

Commandment 1: Be a competent observer of your environment. This is the most basic requirement for anyone wishing to decode and use nonverbal communications.

Imagine the foolishness of trying to listen to someone with plugs in our ears. We couldn't hear the message and whatever was said would be lost on us. Thus, most intent listeners don't go around wearing earplugs! Yet, when it comes to seeing the silent language of nonverbal behavior, many viewers might as well be wearing blindfolds, as oblivious as they are to the body signals around them. Consider this. Just as careful *listening* is critical to understanding our verbal pronouncements, so careful *observation* is vital to comprehending our body language. Whoa! Don't just breeze past that sentence and continue reading. What it states is critical. *Concerted* (effortful) *observation*—is absolutely essential to reading people and detecting their nonverbal tells successfully.

The problem is that most people spend their lives looking but not truly seeing, or, as Sherlock Holmes, the meticulous English detective, declared to his partner, Dr. Watson, "You see, but you do not observe." Sadly, the majority of individuals view their surroundings with a minimal amount of observational effort. Such people are oblivious to subtle changes in their world. They are unaware of the rich tapestry of details that surrounds them, such as the subtle movement of a person's hand or foot that might betray his thoughts or intentions.

In fact, various scientific studies have demonstrated people to be poor observers of their world. For example, when a man dressed in a gorilla suit walked in front of a group of students while other activities were taking place, half the students didn't even notice the gorilla in their midst (Simons & Chabris, 1999, 1059–1074)!

Observation-impoverished individuals lack what airline pilots refer to as "situational awareness," which is a sense of where one is at all times; they don't have a solid mental picture of exactly what is going on around them or even in front of them. Ask them to go into a strange room filled with people, give them a chance to look around, and then tell them to close their eyes and report what they saw. You would be astounded by their inability to recall even the most obvious features in the room.

I find it disheartening how often we run into somebody or read about someone who always seems to be blindsided by life's events. The complaints of these individuals are nearly always the same:

> *"My wife just filed for divorce. I never had a clue she was unhappy with our marriage."*

> *"The guidance counselor tells me my son has been using cocaine for three years. I had no idea he had a drug problem."*

"I was arguing with this guy and out of nowhere he sucker punched me. I never saw it coming."

"I thought the boss was pretty happy with my job performance. I had no idea I was going to be fired."

These are the kinds of statements made by men and women who have never learned how to observe the world around them effectively. Such inadequacies are not surprising, really. After all, as we grow from children to adults, we're never instructed on how to observe the nonverbal clues of others. There are no classes in elementary school, high school, or college that teach people situational awareness. If you're lucky, you teach yourself to be more observant. If you don't, you miss out on an incredible amount of useful information that could help you avoid problems and make your life more fulfilling, be it when dating, at work, or with family.

Fortunately, observation is a skill that can be learned. We don't have to go through life being blindsided. Furthermore, because it is a skill, we can get better at it with the right kind of training and practice. If you are observationally "challenged," do not despair. You can overcome your weakness in this area if you are willing to devote time and effort to observing your world more conscientiously.

What you need to do is make observation—concerted observation—a way of life. Becoming aware of the world around you is not a passive act. It is a conscious, deliberate behavior—something that takes effort, energy, and concentration to achieve, and *constant practice* to maintain. Observation is like a muscle. It grows stronger with use and atrophies without use. Exercise your observation muscle and you will become a more powerful decoder of the world around you.

By the way, when I speak of concerted observation, I am asking you to utilize all your senses, not just your sense of sight. Whenever I walk into my apartment, I take a deep breath. If things don't smell "normal" I become concerned. One time I detected the slight odor of lingering cigarette smoke when I returned home from a trip. My nose alerted me to possible danger well before my eyes could scan my apartment. It turned out that the apartment maintenance man had been by to fix a leaky pipe, and the smoke on his clothes and skin were still lingering in the air several hours later. Fortunately, he was a welcome intruder, but there could just as easily have been a burglar lurking in the next room. The point is, by using all my senses, I was better able to assess my environment and contribute to my own safety and well-being.

Commandment 2: Observing in context is key to understanding nonverbal behavior. When trying to understand nonverbal behavior in real-life situations, the more you understand the *context* in which it takes place, the better you will be at understanding what it means. For example, after a traffic accident, I expect people to be in shock and to walk around looking dazed. I expect their hands to shake and even for them to make poor decisions like walking into oncoming traffic. (This is why officers ask you to stay in your car.) Why? After an accident, people are suffering the effects of a complete hijacking of the "thinking" brain by a region of the brain known as the *limbic system*. The result of this hijacking includes behaviors such as trembling, disorientation, nervousness, and discomfort. In context, these actions are to be expected and confirm the stress from the accident. During a job interview, I expect applicants to be nervous initially and for that nervousness to dissipate. If it shows up again when I ask specific questions, then I have to wonder why these nervous behaviors have suddenly presented again.

Commandment 3: Learn to recognize and decode nonverbal behaviors that are universal. Some body behaviors are considered universal because they are exhibited similarly by most people. For instance, when people press their lips together in a manner that seems to make them disappear, it is a clear and common sign that they are troubled and something is wrong. This nonverbal behavior, known as *lip compression,* is one of the *universal tells* that I will be describing in the chapters to follow (see box 4). The more of these universal nonverbals you can recognize and accurately interpret, the more effective you will be in assessing the thoughts, feelings, and intentions of those around you.

BOX 4: A PURSING OF LIPS LEADS TO SAVINGS ON SHIPS

Universal tells of the lips were very helpful to me during a consulting assignment with a British shipping company. My British client had asked me to sit through their contract negotiations with a huge multinational corporation that would be outfitting their vessels. I agreed and suggested that the proposed contract be presented point by point, with agreement being reached on each item before moving forward. That way I could more closely watch the corporate negotiator for any nonverbals that might reveal information helpful to my client.

"I'll pass you a note if I spot something that needs your attention," I told my client and then settled back to watch the parties review the contract clause by clause. I didn't have long to wait before I saw an important tell. When a clause detailing the outfitting of a specific part of the vessel was read—a construction phase involving millions of dollars—the chief negotiator from the multinational corporation pursed his lips, a clear indication that something in this part of the contract was not to his liking.

I passed a note to my client, warning him that this particular clause in the contract was contentious or problematic and should be revisited and discussed thoroughly while we were all still together.

By confronting the issue then and there—and focusing on the details of the clause in question—the two negotiators were able to hammer out an agreement face-to-face, which ended up saving my client 13.5 million dollars. The negotiator's nonverbal signal of displeasure was the key evidence needed to spot a specific problem and deal with it immediately and effectively.

Commandment 4: Learn to recognize and decode idiosyncratic nonverbal behaviors. Universal nonverbal behaviors constitute one group of body cues: those that are relatively the same for everyone. There is a second type of body cue called an *idiosyncratic nonverbal behavior,* which is a signal that is relatively unique to a particular individual.

In attempting to identify idiosyncratic signals, you'll want to be on the lookout for *behavioral patterns* in people you interact with on a regular basis (friends, family, coworkers, persons who provide goods or services to you on a consistent basis). The better you know an individual, or the longer you interact with him or her, the easier it will be to discover this information because you will have a larger database upon which to make your judgments. For example, if you note your teenager scratches his head and bites his lip when he is about to take a test, this may be a reliable idiosyncratic tell that speaks of his nervousness or lack of preparation. No doubt this has become part of his repertoire for dealing with stress, and you will see it again and again because "the best predictor of future behavior is past behavior."

Commandment 5: When you interact with others, try to establish their baseline behaviors. In order to get a handle on the *baseline behaviors* of the people with whom you regularly interact, you need to note how they look normally, how they typically sit, where they place their hands, the usual position of their feet, their posture and common facial expressions, the tilt of their heads, and even where they generally place or hold their possessions, such as a purse (see figures 1 and 2). You need to be able to differentiate between their "normal" face and their "stressed" face.

Not getting a baseline puts you in the same position as parents who never look down their child's throat until the youngster gets sick. They call the doctor and try to describe what they see inside, but they have no means of making a comparison because they never looked at the child's throat when he or she was healthy. By examining what's normal, we begin to recognize and identify what's abnormal.

Even in a single encounter with someone, you should attempt to note

Fig. 1

Fig. 2

Note features of face when not stressed. Eyes are relaxed and the lips should be full.

A stressed face is tense and slightly contorted, eyebrows are knitted, and the forehead is furrowed.

his or her "starting position" at the beginning of your interaction. Establishing a person's baseline behavior is critical because it allows you to determine when he or she deviates from it, which can be very important and informative (see box 5).

Commandment 6: Always try to watch people for multiple tells—behaviors that occur in clusters or in succession. Your accuracy in reading people will be enhanced when you observe *multiple tells*, or clusters of behavior body signals on which to rely. These signals work together like the parts of a jigsaw puzzle. The more pieces of the puzzle you possess, the better your chances of putting them all together and seeing the picture they portray. To illustrate, if I see a business competitor display a pattern of stress behaviors, followed closely by pacifying behaviors, I can be more confident that she is bargaining from a position of weakness.

Commandment 7: It's important to look for changes in a person's behavior that can signal changes in thoughts, emotions, interest, or intent. Sudden *changes* in behavior can help reveal how a person is

BOX 5: **IT'S A RELATIVE MATTER**

Imagine for a moment that you're the parent of an eight-year-old boy who is waiting in line to greet relatives at a large family reunion. As this is a yearly ritual, you have stood with your son on numerous occasions while he waited his turn to say hello to everyone. He has never hesitated to run up and give family members a big hug. However, on this occasion, when it comes time to embrace his Uncle Harry, he stands stiff and frozen in place.

"What's the matter?" you whisper to him, pushing him toward his waiting uncle.

Your son doesn't say anything, but he is very reluctant to respond to your physical signal.

What should you do? The important thing to note here is that your son's behavior is a deviation from his baseline behavior. In the past, he has never hesitated to greet his uncle with a hug. Why the change in behavior? His "freeze" response suggests he feels threatened or something negative. Perhaps there is no justified reason for his fear, but to the observant and sensibly cautious parent, a warning signal should go off. Your son's deviation from his previous behavior suggests that something negative might have occurred between him and his uncle since their last meeting. Perhaps it was a simple disagreement, the awkwardness of youth, or a reaction to the uncle's preferential treatment of others. Then again, this behavior might indicate something much more sinister. The point is that a change in a person's baseline behavior suggests that something might be amiss and, in this particular case, probably warrants further attention.

processing information or adapting to emotional events. A child who is exhibiting giddiness and delight at the prospect of entering a theme park will change his behavior immediately upon learning the park is closed. Adults are no different. When we get bad news over the phone or see something that can hurt us, our bodies reflect that change immediately.

Changes in a person's behavior can also reveal his or her interest or intentions in certain circumstances. Careful observation of such changes can allow you to predict things before they happen, clearly giving you an advantage—particularly if the impending action could cause harm to you or others (see box 6).

Commandment 8: Learning to detect false or misleading nonverbal signals is also critical. The ability to differentiate between authentic and *misleading cues* takes practice and experience. It requires not only concerted observation, but also some careful judgment. In the chapters to come, I will teach you the subtle differences in a person's actions that reveal whether a behavior is honest or dishonest, increasing your chances of getting an accurate read on the person with whom you are dealing.

Commandment 9: Knowing how to distinguish between comfort and discomfort will help you to focus on the most important behaviors for decoding nonverbal communications. Having studied nonverbal behavior most of my adult life, I have come to realize that there are two principal things we should look for and focus on: *comfort* and *discomfort*. This is fundamental to how I teach nonverbal communications. Learning to read comfort and discomfort cues (behaviors) in others accurately will help you to decipher what their bodies and minds are truly saying. If in doubt as to what a behavior means, ask yourself if this looks like a comfort behavior (e.g., contentment, happiness, relaxation) or if it looks like a discomfort behavior (e.g., displeasure, unhappiness, stress, anxiety, tension). Most of the time you will be able to place observed behaviors in one of these two domains (comfort vs. discomfort).

BOX 6: A NOSE FOR TROUBLE

Among the most important nonverbal clues to a person's thoughts are changes in body language that constitute *intention cues.* These are behaviors that reveal what a person is about to do and provide the competent observer with extra time to prepare for the anticipated action before it takes place.

One personal example of how critical it is to watch for changes in people's behavior—particularly when the changes involve intention cues—involves an attempted robbery of a store where I worked. In this particular situation, I noticed a man standing near the cash register at the checkout counter, a behavior that caught my attention because he seemed to have no reason to be there; he wasn't waiting in line and he hadn't purchased any items. Moreover, the entire time he stood there, his eyes were fixed on the cash register.

If he had just remained quietly where he was, I eventually would have lost interest in him and focused my attention elsewhere. However, while I was still observing him, his behavior changed. Specifically, his nostrils starting flaring (nasal wing dilation), which was a giveaway that he was oxygenating in advance of taking some action. I guessed what that action was going to be about a second before it occurred. And a second was all I had to sound a warning. I yelled to the cashier, "Watch out!" as three things happened at once: (a) the clerk finished ringing up a sale, causing the cash drawer to open; (b) the man near the register lunged forward, plunging his hand into the drawer to grab some cash; and (c) alerted by my shouted warning, the cashier grabbed the man's hand and twisted it, causing the would-be robber to drop the money and run out of the store. Had I not spotted his intention cue, I am sure the thief would have succeeded in his efforts. Incidentally, the cashier was my father, who was running a small hardware store in Miami back in 1974. I was his summer hire.

Commandment 10: When observing others, be subtle about it.
Using nonverbal behavior requires you to observe people carefully and
decode their nonverbal behaviors accurately. However, one thing you
don't want to do when observing others is to make your intentions obvious. Many individuals tend to stare at people when they first try to spot
nonverbal cues. Such intrusive observation is not advisable. Your ideal
goal is to observe others without their knowing it, in other words, unobtrusively.

Work at perfecting your observational skills, and you will reach a
point where your efforts will be both successful *and* subtle. It's all a matter of practice and persistence.

You have now been introduced to your part of our partnership, the
ten commandments you need to follow to decode nonverbal communication successfully. The question now becomes "What nonverbal behaviors
should I be looking for, and what important information do they reveal?" This is where I come in.

Identifying Important Nonverbal Behaviors and Their Meanings

Consider this. The human body is capable of giving off literally thousands of nonverbal "signals" or messages. Which ones are most important and how do you decode them? The problem is that it could take a
lifetime of painstaking observation, evaluation, and validation to identify
and interpret important nonverbal communications accurately. Fortunately, with the help of some very gifted researchers and my practical
experience as an FBI expert on nonverbal behavior, we can take a more
direct approach to get you on your way. I have already identified those
nonverbal behaviors that are most important, so you can put this unique
knowledge to immediate use. We have also developed a paradigm or
model that makes reading nonverbals easier. Even if you forget exactly
what a specific body signal means, you will still be able to decipher it.

As you read through these pages, you will learn certain information
about nonverbal behavior that has never been revealed in any other text

on body language (including examples of nonverbal behavioral clues used to solve actual FBI cases). Some of the material will surprise you. For example, if you had to choose the most "honest" part of a person's body—the part that would most likely reveal an individual's *true* feeling or intentions—which part would you select? Take a guess. Once I reveal the answer, you'll know a prime place to look when attempting to decide what a business associate, family member, date, or total stranger is thinking, feeling, or intending. I will also explain the physiological basis for nonverbal behavior, the role the brain plays in nonverbal behavior. I will also reveal the truth about detecting deception as no counterintelligence agent has done before.

I firmly believe that understanding the biological basis for body language will help you appreciate how nonverbal behavior works and why it is such a potent predictor of human thoughts, feelings, and intentions. Therefore, I start the next chapter with a look at that magnificent organ, the human brain, and show how it governs every facet of our body language. Before I do so, however, I will share an observation concerning the validity of using body language to understand and assess human behavior.

FOR WHOM THE TELLS TOLL

On a fateful date in 1963, in Cleveland, Ohio, thirty-nine-year veteran Detective Martin McFadden watched two men walk back and forth in front of a store window. They took turns peeking into the shop and then walking away. After multiple passes, the two men huddled at the end of the street looking over their shoulders as they spoke to a third person. Concerned that the men were "casing" the business and intending to rob the store, the detective moved in, patted down one of the men, and found a concealed handgun. Detective McFadden arrested the three men, thus thwarting a robbery and averting potential loss of life.

Officer McFadden's detailed observations became the basis for a landmark U.S. Supreme Court decision (*Terry v. Ohio,* 1968, 392 U.S. 1) known to every police officer in the United States. Since 1968, this ruling has allowed police officers to stop and frisk individuals without a warrant when their behaviors telegraph their intention to commit a crime. With this decision, the Supreme Court acknowledged that nonverbal behaviors presage criminality if those behaviors are observed and decoded properly. *Terry v. Ohio* provided a clear demonstration of the relationship between our thoughts, intentions, and nonverbal behaviors. Most important, this decision provided *legal recognition* that such a relationship exists and is valid (Navarro & Schafer, 2003, 22–24).

So the next time someone says to you that nonverbal behavior does not have meaning or is not reliable, remember this case, as it says otherwise and has stood the test of time.

TWO

Living Our Limbic Legacy

Take a moment and bite your lip. Really, take a second and actually do it. Now, rub your forehead. Finally, stroke the back of your neck. These are things we do all the time. Spend some time around other people and you'll see them engaging in these behaviors on a regular basis.

Do you ever wonder *why* they do it? Do you ever wonder why *you* do it? The answer can be found hidden away in a vault—the *cranial vault*—where the human brain resides. Once we learn why and how our brain recruits our body to express its emotions nonverbally, we'll also discover how to interpret these behaviors. So, let's take a closer look inside that vault and examine the most amazing three pounds of matter found in the human body.

Most people think of themselves as having one brain and recognize that brain as the seat of their cognitive abilities. In reality, there are three "brains" inside the human skull, each performing specialized functions that work together as the "command-and-control center" that regulates everything our body does. Back in 1952, a pioneering scientist named Paul MacLean began to speak of the human brain as a *triune brain* consisting of a "reptilian (stem) brain," "mammalian (limbic) brain," and "human (neocortex) brain" (see diagram of the limbic brain). In this book, we will be concentrating on the limbic system of the brain (the part MacLean called the mammalian brain), because it plays the largest role in the expression of our nonverbal behavior. However, we will use our neocortex (our human brain or thinking brain) to analyze critically the limbic reactions of those around us in order to decode what other people are thinking, feeling, or intending (LeDoux, 1996, 184–189; Goleman, 1995, 10–21).

It is critical to understand that the brain controls all behaviors, whether conscious or subconscious. This premise is the cornerstone of understanding all nonverbal communications. From simply scratching your head to composing a symphony, there is nothing you do (except for some involuntary muscle reflexes) that is not governed or directed by the brain. By this

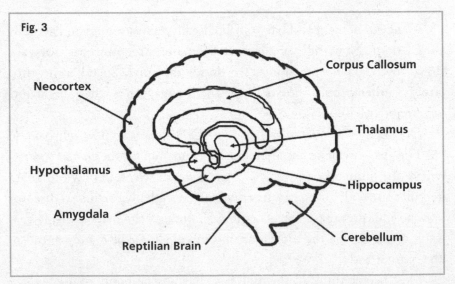

Fig. 3

Corpus Callosum

Neocortex

Thalamus

Hypothalamus

Hippocampus

Amygdala

Cerebellum

Reptilian Brain

Diagram of the limbic brain with major features such as the amygdala and the hippocampus.

logic, we can use these behaviors to interpret what the brain is choosing to communicate externally.

THE VERY ELEGANT LIMBIC BRAIN

In our study of nonverbal communications, the limbic brain is where the action is. Why? Because it is the part of the brain that reacts to the world around us reflexively and instantaneously, in real time, and without thought. For that reason, it gives off a *true* response to information coming in from the environment (Myers, 1993, 35–39). Because it is uniquely responsible for our survival, the limbic brain does not take breaks. It is always "on." The limbic brain is also our emotional center. It is from there that signals go out to various other parts of the brain, which in turn orchestrate our behaviors as they relate to emotions or our survival (LeDoux, 1996, 104–137). These behaviors can be observed and decoded as they manifest physically in our feet, torso, arms, hands, and faces. Since these reactions occur without thought, unlike words, they are genuine. Thus, the limbic brain is considered the "honest brain" when we think of nonverbals (Goleman, 1995, 13–29).

These limbic survival responses go back not only to our own infancy, but also to our ancestry as a human species. They are hardwired into our nervous system, making them difficult to disguise or eliminate—like trying to suppress a startle response even when we anticipate a loud noise. Therefore, it is axiomatic that limbic behaviors are honest and reliable behaviors; they are true manifestations of our thoughts, feelings, and intentions (see box 7).

The third part of our brain is a relatively recent addition to the cranial vault. Thus it is called the *neocortex,* meaning new brain. This part of our brain is also known as the "human," "thinking," or "intellectual" brain, because it is responsible for higher-order cognition and memory. This is the part of the brain that distinguishes us from other mammals due to the large amount of its mass (cortex) used for thinking. This is the brain that got us to the moon. With its ability to compute, analyze,

BOX 7: **HEAD-ING OFF A BOMBER**

Since the limbic part of our brain cannot be cognitively regulated, the behaviors it generates should be given greater importance when interpreting nonverbal communications. You can use your thoughts to try to disguise your true emotions all you want, but the limbic system will self-regulate and give off clues. Observing these alarm reactions and knowing that they are honest and significant is extremely important; it can even save lives.

An example of this occurred in December of 1999, when an alert U.S. customs officer thwarted a terrorist who came to be known as the "millennial bomber." Noting the nervousness and excessive sweating of Ahmed Reesam as he entered the United States from Canada, Officer Diana Dean asked him to step out of his car for further questioning. At that point Reesam attempted to flee but was soon captured. In his car, officers found explosives and timing devices. Reesam was eventually convicted of plotting to bomb the Los Angeles Airport.

The nervousness and sweating that Officer Dean observed were regulated in the brain as a response to immense stress. Because these limbic behaviors are genuine, Officer Dean could be confident in pursuing Reesam, with the knowledge that her observations had detected body language that justified further investigation. The Reesam affair illustrates how one's psychological state manifests nonverbally in the body. In this case, the limbic system of a would-be bomber—who was obviously extremely frightened by the possibility of being detected—gave away his nervousness, despite all conscious attempts he made to hide his underlying emotions. We owe Officer Dean our gratitude for being an astute observer of nonverbal behavior and foiling a terrorist act.

interpret, and intuit at a level unique to the human species, it is our critical and creative brain. It is also, however, the part of the brain that is least honest; therefore, it is our "lying brain." Because it is capable of complex thought, this brain—unlike its limbic counterpart—is the *least* reliable of the three major brain components. This is the brain that can *deceive*, and it deceives often (Vrij, 2003, 1–17).

Returning to our earlier example, while the limbic system may compel the millennial bomber to sweat profusely while being questioned by the customs officer, the neocortex is quite capable of allowing him to lie about his true sentiments. The thinking part of the brain, which is the part that governs our speech (specifically, Broca's area), could cause the bomber to say, "I have no explosives in the car," should the officer inquire as to what is in his automobile, even if that claim is an utter falsehood. The neocortex can easily permit us to tell a friend that we like her new haircut when we, in fact, do not, or it can facilitate the very convincing statement, "I did not have sexual relations with that woman, Ms. Lewinsky."

Because the neocortex (the thinking brain) is capable of dishonesty, it is not a good source of reliable or accurate information (Ost, 2006, 259–291). In summary, when it comes to revealing honest nonverbal behaviors that help us read people, the limbic system is the holy grail of body language. Thus, this is the area of the brain where we want to focus our attention.

OUR LIMBIC RESPONSES—THE THREE F'S OF NONVERBALS

One of the classic ways the limbic brain has assured our survival as a species—and produced a reliable number of nonverbal tells in the process—is by regulating our behavior when confronting danger, whether it be a prehistoric man facing a Stone Age beast or a modern-day employee facing a stone-hearted boss. Over the millennia, we have retained the competent, life-saving visceral reactions of our animal heritage. In order to ensure our survival, the brain's very elegant response to distress or threats, has taken three forms: *freeze, flight,* and *fight.* Like other animal species whose limbic brains protected them in this manner, humans possessing these limbic reactions survived to propagate because these behaviors were already hardwired into our nervous system.

I am sure that many of you are familiar with the phrase "fight-or-flight response," which is common terminology used to describe the way in which we respond to threatening or dangerous situations. Unfortunately, this phrase is only two-thirds accurate and half-assed backward! In reality, the way animals, including humans, react to danger occurs in the following order: freeze, flight, fight. If the reaction really were fight or flight, most of us would be bruised, battered, and exhausted much of the time.

Because we have retained and honed this exquisitely successful process for dealing with stress and danger—and because the resulting reactions generate nonverbal behaviors that help us understand a person's thoughts, feelings, and intentions—it is well worth our time to examine each response in greater detail.

The Freeze Response

A million years ago, as early hominids traversed the African savanna, they were faced with many predators that could outrun and overpower them. For early man to succeed, the limbic brain, which had evolved from our animal forebearers, developed strategies to compensate for the power advantage our predators had over us. That strategy, or first defense of the limbic system, was to use the *freeze response* in the presence of a predator or other danger. Movement attracts attention; by immediately holding still upon sensing a threat, the limbic brain caused us to react in the most effective manner possible to ensure our survival. Most animals, certainly most predators, react to—and are attracted by—movement. This ability to freeze in the face of danger makes sense. Many carnivores go after moving targets and exercise the "chase, trip, and bite" mechanism exhibited by large felines, the primary predators of our ancestors.

Many animals not only freeze their motion when confronted by predators, but some even play dead, which is the ultimate freeze reaction. This is a strategy that opossums use, but they are not the only animals to do so. In fact, accounts of the school shootings at Columbine and Virginia Tech demonstrate that students used the freeze response to deal with deadly predators. By holding still and playing dead, many students survived even though they were only a few feet away from the killer. Instinctively, the students adopted ancient behaviors that work very effectively. Freezing your movement can often make you nearly invisible to others, a phenomenon every soldier and SWAT team operator learns.

Thus, the freeze response has been passed from primitive man to modern man and remains with us today as our first line of defense against a perceived threat or danger. In fact, you can still see this ancient limbic reaction to large felines in the theaters of Las Vegas where big cats are part of the show. As the tiger or lion walks onto the stage, you can be sure that the people in the first row will not be making any unnecessary arm or hand gestures. They will be frozen in their seats. These people were not issued memos to remain still; they did so because the limbic brain has prepared the human species to behave that way in the face of danger for over five million years.

In our modern society, the freeze response is employed more subtly in everyday life. You can observe it when people are caught bluffing or stealing, or sometimes when they are lying. When people feel threatened or exposed, they react just like our ancestors did a million years earlier; they freeze. Not only have we, as humans, learned to freeze in the face of observed or perceived danger, but others around us have learned to copy our behavior and freeze their behavior also, even without seeing the threat. This mimicry or *isopraxism* (same movement) evolved because it was critical to communal survival, as well as social harmony, within the human species (see box 8 on next page).

This freezing action is sometimes termed the "deer-in-the-headlights" effect. When suddenly caught in a potentially dangerous circumstance, we immediately freeze before taking action. In our day-to-day life, this freeze response manifests innocently, such as when a person walking down the street stops suddenly, perhaps hitting himself on the forehead

---

BOX 8: THE NIGHT THE HANDS STOPPED MOVING

I was at my mother's house a few weeks ago watching television and eating ice cream with members of the family. It was late at night and someone rang the doorbell (something that is *very* unusual in her neighborhood). Suddenly, in the midst of eating, everyone's hands froze—adults and children alike—as if choreographed. It was amazing to see how we all reacted with "hands flash frozen" at precisely the same moment. It turned out that the visitor was my sister who had forgotten her keys. But of course we didn't know it was her ringing the bell. It was a beautiful example of the hardwired communal response to perceived danger, and of the first limbic reaction, which is to freeze.

Soldiers in combat react the same way. When the "point man" freezes, everyone freezes; nothing needs to be said.

---

with the palm of his hand, before turning around and heading back to his apartment to turn off the stove. That momentary stop is enough for the brain to do some quick assessing, whether the threat comes in the form of a predator or of a thought remembered. Either way, the psyche must deal with a potentially dangerous situation (Navarro, 2007, 141–163).

We not only freeze when confronted by physical and visual threats, but as in the example of the late-night doorbell, threats from things we hear (aural threats) can also alert the limbic system. For instance, when being chastised, most people hold very still. The same behavior is observed when an individual is being questioned about matters that he or she perceives could get them into trouble. The person will freeze in his chair as if in an "ejector seat" (Gregory, 1999).

A similar manifestation of the limbic freeze occurs during interviews when people hold their breath or their breathing becomes very shallow. Again, this is a very ancient response to a threat. It is not noticed by the interviewee and yet it is quite observable to anyone watching for it. I have often had to tell an interviewee to relax and take a deep breath during the middle of an interview or deposition, as he was unaware of just how shallow his breathing had become.

Consistent with the need to freeze when confronted by a threat, people being questioned about a crime will often fix their feet in a position of security (interlocked behind the chair legs) and hold that position for an inordinate period of time. When I see this type of behavior, it tells me something is wrong; this is a limbic response that needs to be further explored. The person may or may not be lying, since deceit cannot be directly discerned. But I can be assured from their nonverbal behavior that something is stressing them; therefore I will pursue the source of their discomfort through my questioning or interaction.

Another way the limbic brain uses a modification of the freeze response is to attempt to protect us by diminishing our exposure. During surveillance of shoplifters, one of the things that stands out is how often thieves will try to hide their physical presence by restricting their motions or hunching over as if trying to be invisible. Ironically, this makes them stand out even further, since it is such a deviation from normal shopping behavior. Most people walk around a store with their arms quite active and their posture upright rather than stooped. Psychologically, the shoplifters—or, your son and daughter as they try to surreptitiously swipe a cookie from the pantry—are trying to master their environment by attempting to "hide" in the open. Another way people try to hide in the open is by limiting their head exposure. This is done by raising the shoulders and lowering the head—the "turtle effect." Picture a losing football team walking off the field after the game and you get the idea (see figure 4).

Interestingly and sadly, abused children often manifest these freezing limbic behaviors. In the presence of an abusive parent or adult, their arms will go dormant at their sides and they avoid eye contact as though that helps them not to be seen. In a way, they are hiding in the open, which is a tool of survival for these helpless kids.

Fig. 4

The "turtle effect" (shoulders rise toward the ears) is often seen when people are humbled or suddenly lose confidence.

The Flight Response

One purpose of the freeze response is to avoid detection by dangerous predators or in dangerous situations. A second purpose is to give the threatened individual the opportunity to assess the situation and determine the best course of action to take. When the freeze response is not adequate to eliminate the danger or is not the best course of action (e.g., the threat is too close), the second limbic response is to get away by use of the *flight response*. Obviously, the goal of this choice is to escape the threat or, at a minimum, to distance oneself from danger. Running, of course, is useful when it is practical, and as a survival mechanism our brain directed our body to adopt this tactic judiciously over millennia in order to escape from danger.

In our modern world, however, where we live in cities and not in the wild, it is difficult to run from threats; therefore we have adapted the flight response to meet our modern needs. The behaviors are not as obvious, but they serve the same purpose—to either block or distance ourselves from the physical presence of undesirable individuals or things.

If you think back on the social interactions you've had in your life, you'll probably be able to recall some of the "evasive" actions you took to distance yourself from the unwanted attention of others. Just as a child turns away from undesirable food at the dinner table and shifts her feet toward the exit, an individual may turn away from someone she doesn't like, or to avoid conversations that threaten her. Blocking behaviors may manifest in the form of closing the eyes, rubbing the eyes, or placing the hands in front of the face.

The person may also distance herself from someone by leaning away, placing objects (a purse) on her lap, or turning her feet toward the nearest exit. All of these behaviors are controlled by the limbic brain and indicate that someone wants distance from one or more undesirable persons or any perceived threat in the environment. Again, we undertake these behaviors because, for millions of years, humans have withdrawn from things we didn't like or that could harm us. Therefore, to this day, we expedite our exit from a deplorable party, distance ourselves from a bad relationship, or lean away from those who are deemed undesirable or even with whom we strongly disagree (see figure 5).

Just as a man may turn away from his date, an individual in negotiations may shift away from his counterpart if he hears an unattractive offer or feels threatened as bargaining continues. Blocking behaviors may also be manifested; the businessperson may close or rub his eyes, or place his hands in front of his face (see figure 6). He may lean away from the table or the other person and turn his feet away as well, sometimes in the direction of the nearest exit. These are not behaviors of deception, but rather actions that signal that a person feels uncomfortable. These forms of the age-old flight response are *distancing* nonverbal behaviors

People lean away from each other subconsciously when
they disagree or feel uncomfortable around each other.

that tell you the businessperson is unhappy with what is occurring at
the table.

The Fight Response

The *fight response* is the limbic brain's final tactic for survival through aggression. When a person confronting danger cannot avoid detection by
freezing and cannot save himself by distancing or escaping (flight), the
only alternative left is to fight. In our evolution as a species, we—along
with other mammals—developed the strategy of turning fear into rage
in order to fight off attackers (Panksepp, 1998, 208). In the modern

Eye blocking is a very powerful display of
consternation, disbelief, or disagreement.

world, however, acting on our rage may not be practical or even legal, so
the limbic brain has developed other strategies beyond the more primitive physical fight response.

One form of modern aggression is an argument. Although the original meaning of the term *argument* relates simply to a debate or discussion, the word is increasingly used to describe a verbal altercation. An
overheated argument is essentially "fighting" by nonphysical means. The
use of insults, ad hominem phrases, counterallegations, denigration of
professional stature, goading, and sarcasm are all, in their own ways, the
modern equivalents of fighting, because they are all forms of aggression.
If you think about it, civil lawsuits can even be construed as a modern
and socially sanctioned type of fight or aggression in which litigants aggressively argue two opposing viewpoints.

While humans probably engage in physical altercations far less now
than in other periods in our history, fighting is still a part of our limbic
armory. Although some people are more prone to violence than others,
our limbic response shows up in many ways other than punching, kicking, and biting. You can be very aggressive without physical contact, for
example, just by using your posture, your eyes, by puffing out your chest,

or by violating another's personal space. Threats to our personal space elicit a limbic response on an individual level. Interestingly, these territorial violations can also create limbic responses on a collective level. When one country intrudes into the space of another, it often results in economic sanctions, severing of diplomatic relations, or even wars.

Obviously, it is easy to recognize when someone uses the fight response to commit a physical assault. What I want to identify for you are the not-so-obvious ways in which individuals exhibit some of the more subtle behaviors associated with the fight response. Just as we have seen modified expressions of the freeze and flight limbic reactions, modern decorum dictates that we refrain from acting on our primitive inclinations to fight when threatened.

In general, I advise people to refrain from using aggression (verbal or physical) as a means of achieving their objectives. Just as the fight response is the act of last resort in dealing with a threat—used only after the freeze and flight tactics have proven unworkable—so too should you avoid it whenever feasible. Aside from the obvious legal and physical reasons for this recommendation, aggressive tactics can lead to emotional turmoil, making it difficult to concentrate and think clearly about the threatening situation at hand. When we are emotionally aroused—and a good fight will do that—it affects our ability to think effectively. This happens because our cognitive abilities are hijacked so that the limbic brain can have full use of all available cerebral resources (Goleman, 1995, 27, 204–207). One of the best reasons for studying nonverbal behaviors is that they can sometimes warn you when a person intends to harm you physically, giving you time to avoid a potential conflict.

COMFORT/DISCOMFORT AND PACIFIERS

To borrow a phrase from the old *Star Trek* series, the "prime directive" of the limbic brain is to ensure our survival as a species. It does this by being programmed to make us secure by avoiding danger or discomfort and seeking safety or comfort whenever possible. It also allows us to remember experiences from our past encounters and build upon them (see box 9). Thus far we have seen how efficiently the limbic system helps us to deal with threats. Now let's look at how our brain and body work together to comfort us and give us confidence in our personal safety.

When we experience a sense of comfort (well-being), the limbic brain "leaks" this information in the form of body language congruent with our positive feelings. Observe someone resting in a hammock on a breezy day. His body reflects the high comfort being experienced by his brain. On the other hand, when we feel distressed (discomfort), the limbic brain expresses nonverbal behavior that mirrors our negative state of being. Just watch people at the airport when a flight is canceled or delayed. Their bodies say it all. Therefore, we want to learn to look more closely at the comfort and discomfort behaviors we see every day and use them to assess for feelings, thoughts, and intentions.

In general, when the limbic brain is in a state of comfort, this mental and physiological well-being is reflected in nonverbal displays of contentment and *high confidence*. When, however, the limbic brain is experiencing discomfort, the corresponding body language is characterized by behaviors emblematic of stress or *low confidence*. Knowledge of these "behavioral markers" or tells will help you determine what a person may be thinking, or how to act or what to expect when dealing with other people in any social or work context.

The Importance of Pacifying Behaviors

Understanding how the limbic system's freeze, flight, and fight responses influence nonverbal behavior is only part of the equation. As you study nonverbal behavior, you will discover that whenever there is a limbic response—especially to a negative or threatening experience—it will be followed by what I call *pacifying behaviors* (Navarro, 2007, 141–163).

These actions, often referred to in the literature as *adapters*, serve to calm us down after we experience something unpleasant or downright nasty (Knapp & Hall, 2002, 41–42). In its attempt to restore itself to "normal conditions," the brain enlists the body to provide comforting

BOX 9: **A BRAIN THAT DOESN'T FORGET**

The limbic brain is like a computer that receives and retains data from the outside world. In doing so, it compiles and maintains a record of negative events and experiences (a burned finger from a hot stove, an assault by a human or animal predator, or even hurtful comments) as well as pleasant encounters. Using this information, the limbic brain allows us to navigate a dangerous and often unforgiving world (Goleman, 1995, 10–21). For example, once the limbic system registers an animal as dangerous, that impression becomes embedded in our emotional memory so that the next time we see that animal, we will react instantly. Likewise, if we run into the "class bully" twenty years later, negative feelings of long ago will percolate to the surface once more, thanks to the limbic brain.

The reason it is often difficult to forget when someone has hurt us is because that experience registers in the more primitive limbic system, which is the part of the brain designed not to reason but to react (Goleman, 1995, 207). I recently encountered an individual with whom I was never on the best of terms. It had been four years since I had last seen this person, yet my visceral (limbic) reactions were just as negative as they had been years ago. My brain was reminding me that this individual takes advantage of others, so it was warning me to stay away. This phenomenon is precisely what Gavin de Becker was talking about in his insightful book, *The Gift of Fear*.

Conversely, the limbic system also works efficiently to register and retain a record of positive events and experiences (e.g., satisfaction of basic needs, praise, and enjoyable interpersonal relationships). Thus, a friendly or familiar face will cause an immediate reaction—a sense of pleasure and well-being. The feelings of euphoria when we see an old friend or recognize a pleasant smell from childhood occur because those encounters have been registered in the "comfort zone" of the memory bank associated with our limbic system.

(pacifying) behaviors. Since these are outward signals that can be read in real time, we can observe and decode them immediately and in context.

Pacifying is not unique to our species. For example, cats and dogs lick themselves and each other to pacify. Humans engage in much more diverse pacification behaviors. Some are very obvious, while others are much more subtle. Most people would readily think of a child's thumb sucking when asked to identify a pacifying behavior, but do not realize that after we outgrow that comfort display, we adopt more discreet and socially acceptable ways to satisfy the need to calm ourselves (e.g., chewing gum, biting pencils). Most people don't notice the more subtle pacifying behaviors or are unaware of their significance in revealing a person's thoughts and feelings. That is unfortunate. To be successful at reading nonverbal behavior, learning to recognize and decode human pacifiers is absolutely critical. Why? Because pacifying behaviors reveal so much about a person's current state of mind, and they do so with uncanny accuracy (see box 10).

I look for pacifying behaviors in people to tell me when they are not at ease or when they are reacting negatively to something I have done or said. In an interview situation, such a display might be in response to a specific question or comment. Behaviors that signal discomfort (e.g., leaning away, a frown, and crossed or tense arms) are usually followed by the brain enlisting the hands to pacify (see figure 8). I look for these behaviors to confirm what is going on in the mind of the person with whom I am dealing.

As a specific example, if every time I ask a subject, "Do you know Mr. Hillman?" he responds, "No," but then immediately touches his neck or mouth, I know he is pacifying to that specific question (see figure 9). I don't know if he is lying, because deception is notoriously difficult to detect. But I do know that he is bothered by the inquiry, so much so that he has to pacify himself after he hears it. This will prompt me to probe further into this area of inquiry. Pacifying behaviors are important for an investigator to note, since sometimes they help uncover a lie or hidden information. I find pacifying indicators of greater significance and reliability than trying to establish veracity. They help to identify what specific

BOX 10: CAPTURED IN THE NECK OF TIME

Neck touching and/or stroking is one of the most significant and frequent pacifying behaviors we use in responding to stress. When women pacify using the neck, they often do so by covering or touching their *suprasternal notch* with their hand (see figure 7). The suprasternal notch is the hollow area between the Adam's apple and the breastbone that is sometimes referred to as the *neck dimple.* When a woman touches this part of her neck and/or covers it with her hand, it is typically because she feels distressed, threatened, uncomfortable, insecure, or fearful. This is a relatively significant behavioral clue that can be used to detect, among other things, the discomfort experienced when a person is lying or concealing important information.

I once worked on an investigation where we thought an armed and dangerous fugitive might be hiding out at his mother's home. Another agent and I went to the woman's house, and when we knocked at the door, she agreed to let us in. We showed our identification and began asking her a series of questions. When I inquired, "Is your son in the house?" she put her hand to her suprasternal notch and said, "No, he's not." I noted her behavior, and we continued with our questioning. After a few minutes I asked, "Is it possible that while you were at work, your son could have sneaked into the house?" Once again, she put her hand up to her neck dimple and replied, "No, I'd know that." I was now confident that her son was in the house, because the only time she moved her hand to her neck was when I suggested that possibility. To make absolutely sure my assumption was correct, we continued to speak with the woman until, as we prepared to leave, I made one last inquiry. "Just so I can finalize my records, you're *positive* he's not in the house, right?" For a third time, her hand went to her neck as she affirmed her earlier answer. I was now certain the woman was lying. I asked for permission to search the house and, sure enough, her son was hiding in a closet under some blankets. She was lucky she was not charged with obstruction of justice. Her discomfort in lying to the police about her fugitive son caused her limbic system to generate a pacifying behavior that tipped her hand and gave her away.

subjects trouble or distress a person. Knowing these can often lead to evincing information previously hidden that might give us new insights.

Types of Pacifying Behaviors

Pacifying behaviors take many forms. When stressed, we might soothe our necks with a gentle massage, stroke our faces, or play with our hair. This is done automatically. Our brains send out the message, "Please pacify me now," and our hands respond immediately, providing an action that will help make us comfortable again. Sometimes we pacify by rubbing our cheeks or our lips from the inside with our tongues, or we exhale slowly

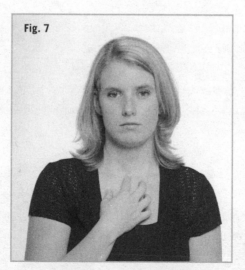

Fig. 7

Covering of the neck dimple pacifies insecurities, emotional discomfort, fear, or concerns in real time. Playing with a necklace often serves the same purpose.

Fig. 8

Rubbing of the forehead is usually a good indicator that a person is struggling with something or is undergoing slight to severe discomfort.

Fig. 9

Neck touching takes place when there is emotional discomfort, doubt, or insecurity.

Cheek or face touching is a way to pacify when nervous, irritated, or concerned.

Exhaling with puffed out cheeks is a great way to release stress and to pacify. Notice how often people do this after a near mishap.

with puffed cheeks to calm ourselves (see figures 10 and 11). If a stressed person is a smoker, he or she will smoke more; if the person chews gum, he or she will chew faster. All these pacifying behaviors satisfy the same requirement of the brain; that is, the brain requires the body to do something that will stimulate nerve endings, releasing calming endorphins in the brain, so that the brain can be soothed (Panksepp, 1998, 272).

For our purposes, any touching of the face, head, neck, shoulder, arm, hand, or leg in response to a negative stimulus (e.g., a difficult question, an embarrassing situation, or stress as a result of something heard, seen, or thought) is a pacifying behavior. These stroking behaviors don't help us to solve problems; rather, they help us to remain calm while we do. In other words, they soothe us. Men prefer to touch their faces. Women prefer to touch their necks, clothing, jewelry, arms, and hair.

When it comes to pacifiers, people have personal favorites, some choose to chew gum, smoke cigarettes, eat more food, lick their lips, rub their chins, stroke their faces, play with objects (pens, pencils, lipstick, or watches), pull their hair, or scratch their forearms. Sometimes pacification is even more subtle, like a person brushing the front of his shirt or adjusting his tie (see figure 12). He appears simply to be preening himself, but in

Fig. 12

Men adjust their ties to deal with insecurities or discomfort. It also covers the suprasternal notch.

reality he is calming his nervousness by drawing his arm across his body and giving his hands something to do. These, too, are pacifying behaviors ultimately governed by the limbic system and exhibited in response to stress.

Below are some of the most common and pronounced pacifying behaviors. When you see them, stop and ask yourself, "Why is this person pacifying?" The ability to link a pacifying behavior with the specific stressor that caused it can help you understand a person's thoughts, feelings, and intentions more accurately.

Pacifying Behaviors Involving the Neck

Neck touching and/or stroking is one of the most significant and frequent pacifying behaviors we use in responding to stress. One person may rub or massage the back of his neck with his fingers; another may stroke the sides of his neck or just under the chin above the Adam's apple, tugging at the fleshy area of the neck. This area is rich with nerve endings that, when stroked, reduce blood pressure, lower the heart rate, and calm the individual down (see figures 13 and 14).

Fig. 13

Fig. 14

Men tend to massage or stroke their necks to pacify distress. This area is rich with nerves, including the vagus nerve, which when massaged will slow down the heart rate.

Men typically cover their necks more robustly than women as a way to deal with discomfort or insecurity.

Over the decades that I have studied nonverbal behaviors, I have observed that there are gender differences in the way men and women use the neck to pacify themselves. Typically, men are more robust in their pacifying behaviors, grasping or cupping their necks just beneath the chin with their hands, thereby stimulating the nerves (specifically, the vagus nerves or the carotid sinus) of the neck, which in turn slow the heart rate down and have a calming effect. Sometimes men will stroke the sides or the back of the neck with their fingers, or adjust their tie knot or shirt collar (see figure 15).

Women pacify differently. For example, when women pacify using the neck, they will sometimes touch, twist, or otherwise manipulate a necklace, if they are wearing one (see box 11). As mentioned, the other major way women neck pacify is by covering their suprasternal notch with their hand. Women touch their hands to this part of their neck and/ or cover it when they feel stressed, insecure, threatened, fearful, uncomfortable, or anxious. Interestingly, when a woman is pregnant, I have observed that her hand will initially move toward her neck but at the last moment will divert to her belly, as if to cover the fetus.

BOX 11: **THE PACIFYING PENDULUM**

Watch a couple as they converse at a table. If the woman begins to play with her necklace, most likely she is a little nervous. But if she transitions her fingers to her neck dimple (suprasternal notch), chances are there is an issue of concern to her or she feels very insecure. In most instances, if she is using her right hand on her suprasternal notch, she will cup her right elbow with her left hand. When the stressful situation is over or there is an intermission in the uncomfortable part of the discussion, her right hand will lower and relax across her folded left arm. If the situation again becomes tense, her right hand will rise, once again, to the suprasternal notch. From a distance, the arm movement looks like the needle on a stress meter, moving from resting (on the arm) to the neck (upright) and back again, according to the level of stress experienced.

Fig. 15

Even a brief touch of the neck will serve to assuage anxiety or discomfort. Neck touching or massaging is a powerful and universal stress reliever and pacifier.

Pacifying Behaviors Involving the Face

Touching or stroking the face is a frequent human pacifying response to stress. Motions such as rubbing the forehead; touching, rubbing, or licking the lip(s); pulling or massaging the earlobe with thumb and forefinger; stroking the face or beard; and playing with the hair all can serve to pacify an individual when confronting a stressful situation. As mentioned before, some individuals will pacify by puffing out their cheeks and then slowly exhaling. The plentiful supply of nerve endings in the face make it an ideal area of the body for the limbic brain to recruit to comfort itself.

Pacifying Behaviors Involving Sounds

Whistling can be a pacifying behavior. Some people whistle to calm themselves when they are walking in a strange area of a city or down a dark, deserted corridor or road. Some people even talk to themselves in an attempt to pacify during times of stress. I have a friend (as I am sure we all do) who can talk a mile a minute when nervous or upset. Some behaviors combine tactile and auditory pacification, such as the tapping of a pencil or the drumming of fingers.

Excessive Yawning

Sometimes we see individuals under stress yawning excessively. Yawning not only is a form of "taking a deep breath," but during stress, as the mouth gets dry, a yawn can put pressure on the salivary glands. The stretch of various structures in and around the mouth causes the glands to release moisture into a dry mouth during times of anxiety. In these cases it's not lack of sleep, but rather stress, that causes the yawning.

The Leg Cleanser

Leg cleansing is one pacification behavior that often goes unnoticed because it frequently occurs under a desk or table. In this calming or pacifying activity, a person places the hand (or hands) palm down on top of the leg (or legs), and then slides them down the thighs toward the knee (see figure 16). Some individuals will do the "leg cleanser" only once, but often it is done repeatedly or the leg merely is massaged. It may also be done to dry off sweaty palms associated with anxiety, but principally it is to get rid of tension. This nonverbal behavior is worth looking for, because it is a good indication that someone is under stress. One way to try and spot this

Fig. 16

When stressed or nervous, people will "cleanse" their palms on their laps in order to pacify themselves. Often missed under tables, it is a very accurate indicator of discomfort or anxiety.

behavior is to watch people who put one or both arms under the table. If they are doing leg cleansing, you will normally see the upper arm and shoulder moving in conjunction with the hand as it rubs along their leg.

In my experience, I find the leg cleanser to be very significant because it occurs so quickly in reaction to a negative event. I have observed this action for years in cases when suspects are presented with damning evidence, such as pictures of a crime scene with which they are already familiar (guilty knowledge). This *cleansing/pacifying behavior* accomplishes two things at once. It dries sweaty palms and pacifies through tactile stroking. You can also see it when a seated couple is bothered or interrupted by an unwelcome intruder, or when someone is struggling to remember a name.

In police work, watch for the hand/leg pacifiers to appear when the interview session starts, and then note if they progressively increase when difficult questions arise. An increase in either the number or vigor of leg cleansers is a very good indicator that a question has caused some sort of discomfort for the person, either because he has guilty knowledge, is lying, or because you are getting close to something he does not want to discuss (see box 12). The behavior might also occur because the interviewee is distressed over what he is required to answer in response to our questions. So, keep an eye on what goes on under the table by monitoring the movement of the arms. You will be surprised at how much you can glean from these behaviors.

Heed this cautionary note about leg cleansing. While it is certainly seen in people who are being deceptive, I have also observed it in innocent individuals who are merely nervous, so be careful not to jump to any conclusions too quickly (Frank et al., 2006, 248–249). The best way to interpret a leg cleanser is to recognize that it reflects the brain's need to pacify and, therefore, the reasons for the individual's behavior should be investigated further.

The Ventilator

This behavior involves a person (usually a male) putting his fingers between his shirt collar and neck and pulling the fabric away from his

---

BOX 12: FROM FACEBOOK TO DISGRACEBOOK

During an interview for a job, an applicant was being questioned by his prospective employer. Everything was going well until, toward the end of the interview, the candidate began talking about networking and the importance of the Internet. The employer complimented him on this comment and made an offhand remark about how most college graduates used the Internet to network in a destructive way, using sites like Facebook to post messages and pictures that would prove to be an embarrassment later in the person's life. At that point, the employer noticed that the candidate did a vigorous leg cleansing with his right hand, wiping it along his thigh several times. The employer said nothing at the time, thanked the young man for the interview, and walked him out of the office. He then returned to his computer—his suspicion aroused by the candidate's pacifying behavior—and checked to see if the young man's profile was on Facebook. Sure enough, it was. And it was not flattering!

---

skin (see figure 17). This *ventilating action* is often a reaction to stress and is a good indicator that the person is unhappy with something he is thinking about or experiencing in his environment. A woman may perform this nonverbal activity more subtly by merely ventilating the front of her blouse or by tossing the back of her hair up in the air to ventilate her neck.

The Self-Administered Body-Hug

When facing stressful circumstances, some individuals will pacify by crossing their arms and rubbing their hands against their shoulders, as if experiencing a chill. Watching a person employ this pacifying behavior is reminiscent of the way a mother hugs a young child. It is a protective and calming action we adopt to pacify ourselves when we want to

Fig. 17

Ventilating of the neck area relieves stress and emotional discomfort. Rodney Dangerfield, the comedian, was famous for doing this when he wasn't getting any "respect."

feel safe. However, if you see a person with his arms crossed in front, leaning forward, and giving you a defiant look, this is *not* a pacifying behavior!

USING PACIFIERS TO READ PEOPLE MORE EFFECTIVELY

In order to gain knowledge about a person through nonverbal pacifiers, there are a few guidelines you need to follow:

(1) Recognize pacifying behaviors when they occur. I have provided you with all of the major pacifiers. As you make a concerted effort to spot these body signals, they will become increasingly easy to recognize in interactions with other people.

(2) Establish a pacifying baseline for an individual. That way you can note any increase and/or intensity in that person's pacifying behaviors and react accordingly.

(3) When you see a person make a pacifying gesture, stop and ask yourself, "What caused him to do that?" You know the individual feels uneasy about something. Your job, as a collector of nonverbal intelligence, is to find out what that something is.

(4) Understand that pacifying behaviors almost always are used to calm a person after a stressful event occurs. Thus, as a general principle, you can assume that if an individual is engaged in pacifying behavior, some stressful event or stimulus has preceded it and caused it to happen.

(5) The ability to link a pacifying behavior with the specific stressor that caused it can help you better understand the person with whom you are interacting.

(6) In certain circumstances you can actually say or do something to see if it stresses an individual (as reflected in an increase in pacifying behaviors) to better understand his thoughts and intentions.

(7) Note what part of the body a person pacifies. This is significant, because the higher the stress, the greater the amount of facial or neck stroking is involved.

(8) Remember, the greater the stress or discomfort, the greater the likelihood of pacifying behaviors to follow.

Pacifiers are a great way to assess for comfort and discomfort. In a sense, pacifying behaviors are "supporting players" in our limbic reactions. Yet they reveal much about our emotional state and how we are truly feeling.

A FINAL NOTE ON OUR LIMBIC LEGACY

You now are in possession of information that is unknown to most people. You are aware that we have a very robust survival mechanism (freeze, flight, or fight) and possess a pacifying system to deal with stress. We are fortunate to have these mechanisms, not only for our own survival and success, but also to use in assessing the sentiments and thoughts of others.

In this chapter, we also learned that (with the exception of certain reflexes) all behavior is governed by the brain. We have examined two of the three major "brains" within our cranial vault—the thinking neocortex brain and the more automatic limbic brain—and how they differ in terms of their roles. Both brains perform important functions. However, for our purposes, the limbic system is more important because it is the most honest brain—responsible for producing the most significant non-verbal signals for determining true thoughts and feelings (Ratey, 2001, 147–242).

Now that you are familiar with the basics of how the brain reacts to the world, you might be wondering if detecting and decoding nonverbal behaviors is all that easy to do. This is a frequently asked question. The answer is yes and no. Once you've read this book, some nonverbal body cues will stand out. They literally scream for attention. On the other hand, there are many aspects of body language that are more subtle and, therefore, more difficult to spot. We will focus on both the more obvious and the more subtle behaviors that the limbic brain elicits from the body. In time and with practice, decoding them will become natural, like looking both ways before you cross a busy street. This brings us to our legs and feet, which propel us across the intersection and provide the focal point of our attention in the next chapter.

THREE

Getting a Leg Up on Body Language

Nonverbals of the Feet and Legs

In the first chapter, I asked you to guess which is the most honest part of the body—the part that is most likely to reveal a person's true intentions and, thus, be a prime place to look for nonverbal signals that accurately reflect what he or she is thinking. It may surprise you, but the answer is the feet! That's right, your feet, along with your legs, win the honesty award hands—or should I say—feet down.

Now I will explain how to gauge the sentiments and intentions of others by focusing on their foot and leg actions. In addition, you will learn to look for telltale signs that help disclose what's going on under the table, even when you can't directly watch the lower limbs. First, however, I want to share with you why your feet are the most honest part of your body, so you'll gain a better appreciation for why the feet are such good gauges of people's true sentiments and intentions.

AN EVOLUTIONARY "FOOT" NOTE

For millions of years, the feet and legs have been the primary means of locomotion for the human species. They are the principal means by which we have maneuvered, escaped, and survived. Since the time our ancestors began to walk upright across the grasslands of Africa, the human foot has carried us, quite literally, around the world. Marvels of engineering, our feet allow us to feel, walk, turn, run, swivel, balance, kick, climb, play, grasp, and even write. And while not as efficient at certain tasks as our hands (we lack an opposable big toe), nevertheless, as Leonardo da Vinci once commented, our feet and what they can perform are a testament to exquisite engineering (Morris, 1985, 239).

The writer and zoologist Desmond Morris observed that our feet communicate exactly what we think and feel more honestly than any other part of our bodies (Morris, 1985, 244). Why are the feet and legs such accurate reflectors of our sentiments? For millions of years, long before humans spoke, our legs and feet reacted to environmental threats (e.g., hot sand, meandering snakes, ill-tempered lions) instantaneously, without the need for conscious thought. Our limbic brains made sure that our feet and legs reacted as needed by either ceasing motion, running away, or kicking at a potential threat. This survival regimen, retained from our ancestral heritage, has served us well and continues to do so today. In fact, these age-old reactions are still so hardwired in us that when we are presented with something dangerous or even disagreeable, our feet and legs still react as they did in prehistoric times. First they freeze, then they attempt to distance, and finally, if no other alternative is available, they prepare to fight and kick.

This freeze, flight, or fight mechanism requires no high-order cognitive processing. It is reactive. This important evolutionary development benefited the individual as well as the group. Humans survived by seeing and responding to the same threat simultaneously or by reacting to the vigilant actions of others and behaving accordingly. When the group was threatened, whether or not they all saw the danger, they were able to react in synchrony by noting each other's movements. In our contemporary world, soldiers on patrol will fix their attention on the "point man." When he freezes, they all freeze. When he lunges for the side of the road, they also take cover. When he charges an ambush, they react in kind. With regard to these life-saving group behaviors, little has changed in five million years.

This ability to communicate nonverbally has assured our survival as a species, and even though today we often cover our legs with clothing and our feet with shoes, our lower limbs still react—not only to threats and stressors—but also to emotions, both negative *and* positive. Thus, our feet and legs transmit information about what we are sensing, thinking, and feeling. The dancing and jumping up and down we do today are extensions of the celebratory exuberance people exhibited millions of years ago upon the completion of a successful hunt. Be they Masai warriors jumping high in place or couples dancing up a storm, throughout the world, the feet and legs communicate happiness. We even stomp our feet in unison at ball games to let our team know we are rooting for them.

Other evidence of these "foot feelings" abounds in our everyday life. For example, watch children and their foot movements for a real education in feet honesty. A child may be sitting down to eat, but if she wants to go out and play, notice how her feet sway, how they stretch to reach the floor from a high chair even when the child is not yet finished with her meal. A parent may try to keep her in place, yet the girl's feet will inch away from the table. Her torso may be held by that loving parent, but the youngster will twist and squirm her legs and feet ever so diligently in the direction of the door—an accurate reflection of where she wants to go. This is an intention cue. As adults, we are, of course, more restrained in these limbic exhibitions, but just barely so.

THE MOST HONEST PART OF OUR BODY

When reading body language, most individuals start their observation at the top of a person (the face) and work their way down, despite the fact that the face is the one part of the body that most often is used to bluff and conceal true sentiments. My approach is the exact opposite. Having conducted thousands of interviews for the FBI, I learned to concentrate on the suspect's feet and legs first, moving upward in my observations until I read the face last. When it comes to honesty, truthfulness *decreases* as we move from the feet to the head. Unfortunately, law enforcement literature over the last sixty years, including some contemporary works, has emphasized a facial focus when conducting interviews or attempting to read people. Further complicating an honest read is the fact that most interviewers compound the problem by allowing the interviewees to conceal their feet and legs under tables and desks.

When you give it some thought, there's good reason for the deceitful nature of our facial expressions. We lie with our faces because that's what we've been taught to do since early childhood. "Don't make that face," our parents growl when we honestly react to the food placed in front of us. "At least *look* happy when your cousins stop by," they instruct, and you learn to force a smile. Our parents—and society—are, in essence, telling us to hide, deceive, and lie with our faces for the sake of social harmony. So it is no surprise that we tend to get pretty good at it, so good, in fact, that when we put on a happy face at a family gathering, we might look as if we love our in-laws when, in reality, we are fantasizing about how to hasten their departure.

Think about it. If we *couldn't* control our facial expressions, why would the term *poker face* have any meaning? We know how to put on a so-called party face, but few pay any attention to their own feet and legs, much less to those of others. Nervousness, stress, fear, anxiety, caution, boredom, restlessness, happiness, joy, hurt, shyness, coyness, humility, awkwardness, confidence, subservience, depression, lethargy, playfulness, sensuality, and anger can all manifest through the feet and legs. A meaningful touch of the legs between lovers, the shy feet of a young boy meeting strangers, the stance of the angry, the nervous pacing of an expectant father—all of these signal our emotional state and can be readily observed in real time.

If you want to decode the world around you and interpret behavior accurately, watch the feet and the legs; they are truly remarkable and honest in the information they convey. The lower limbs must be viewed as a significant part of the entire body when collecting nonverbal intelligence.

SIGNIFICANT NONVERBAL BEHAVIORS INVOLVING THE FEET AND LEGS

Happy Feet

Happy feet are feet and legs that wiggle and/or bounce with joy. When people suddenly display happy feet—particularly if this occurs right after they have heard or seen something of significance—it's because it has affected them in a positive emotional way. Happy feet are a *high-confidence tell*, a signal that a person feels he is getting what he wants or is in an advantageous position to gain something of value from another person or from something else in his environment (see box 13). Lovers seeing each other after a long separation will get happy feet at their airport reunion.

You don't need to look under the table to see happy feet. Just look at a person's shirt and/or his shoulders. If his feet are wiggling or bouncing, his shirt and shoulders will be vibrating or moving up and down. These are not grossly exaggerated movements; in fact, they are relatively subtle. But if you watch for them, they are discernible.

Try this little demonstration for yourself. Sit in a chair in front of a full-length mirror and begin wiggling or bouncing your feet. As you do, you'll start to see your shirt and/or shoulders move. While with others, if you're not watching carefully above the table for these telltale signs of lower-limb behaviors, you might miss them. But if you're willing to take the time and effort to look, you'll be able to detect them. The key to using happy feet as an effective nonverbal signal is first to note a person's foot behavior, and then to watch for any sudden changes that take place (see box 14 on page 59).

Allow me to express two points of caution. First, as with all nonverbal behavior, happy feet must be taken in context to determine if

BOX 13: **HAPPY FEET MEAN LIFE IS SWEET**

A while back, I was watching a poker tournament on television and I saw a guy dealt a flush (a powerful hand). Below the table, his feet were going wild! They were wiggling and bouncing like the feet of a child who's just learned he's going to Disney World. The player's face was stoic, his demeanor above the table was calm, but down near the floor there was a whole lot of shakin' goin' on! Meanwhile, I was pointing at the TV set and urging the other players to fold their hands and get out of the game. Too bad they couldn't hear me, because two players called his bets and lost their money to his unbeatable hand.

This player has learned how to put on his best poker face. Obviously, however, he has a long way to go when it comes to putting on his best poker feet. Fortunately for him, his opponents—like most people—have spent a lifetime ignoring three-quarters of the human body (from the chest on down), paying no attention to the critical nonverbal tells that can be found there.

Poker rooms aren't the only place where you see happy feet. I have seen them in plenty of meeting rooms and boardrooms and just about everywhere else. While writing this chapter, I was at the airport and overheard a young mother sitting next to me as she was talking on her cell phone to members of her family. At first, her feet were flat on the ground, but when her son got on the phone, her feet began bouncing up and down effusively. I did not need her to tell me how she felt about her child or his priority in her life. Her feet shouted it to me.

Remember, whether you are playing cards, doing business, or simply are engaged in a conversation with friends, happy feet are one of the most honest ways our brains truthfully exclaim, "I am elated."

BOX 14: **A SIGN OF THE FEET**

Julie, a human resource executive for a major corporation, told me she began noticing foot behaviors after attending one of my seminars for bank executives. She put her new knowledge to good use just a few days after returning to her job. "I was responsible for selecting company employees for overseas assignments," she explained. "When I asked one potential candidate if she wanted to work abroad, she responded with bouncing, happy feet and an affirmative, 'Yes!' However, when I next mentioned that the destination was Mumbai, India, her feet stopped moving altogether. Noting the change in her nonverbal behavior, I asked why she didn't want to go there. The candidate was astounded. 'Is it that noticeable? I didn't say *anything*. Did someone else say something to you?' she asked in a startled voice. I told the woman I could 'sense' she wasn't pleased with the intended work location. 'You're right,' she admitted, 'I thought I was being considered for Hong Kong, where I have a few friends.' It was obvious she did not want to go to India, and her feet left no doubt about her feelings on the matter."

---

they represent a true tell or just excess nervous behavior. For example, if a person has naturally jittery legs (a kind of restless-leg syndrome), then it might be hard to distinguish happy feet from an individual's normal nervous energy. If the rate or intensity of jiggling increases, however, particularly right after a person hears or witnesses something of significance, I might view that as a potential signal that he or she now feels more confident and satisfied with the current state of affairs.

Second, moving feet and legs may simply signify impatience. Our feet often jiggle or bounce when we grow impatient or feel the need to move things along. Watch a class full of students and notice how often their legs and feet will twitch, jiggle, move, and kick throughout the class. This activity usually increases as the class draws to a close. More often than not, this is a good indicator of impatience and the need to speed things up, *not* a sign of happy feet. Such activity reaches a crescendo as dismissal time approaches in my classes. Perhaps the students are trying to tell me something.

When Feet Shift Direction, Particularly Toward or Away from a Person or Object

We tend to turn toward things we like or are agreeable to us, and that includes individuals with whom we are interacting. In fact, we can use this information to determine whether others are happy to see us or would prefer that we leave them alone. Assume you are approaching two people engaged in a conversation. These are individuals you have met before, and you want to join in the discussion, so you walk up to them and say "hi." The problem is that you're not sure if they really want your company. Is there a way to find out? Yes. Watch their feet and torso behavior. If they move their feet—along with their torsos—to admit you, then the welcome is full and genuine. However, if they don't move their feet to welcome you but, instead, only swivel at the hips to say hello, then they'd rather be left alone.

We tend to turn away from things that we don't like or that are disagreeable to us. Studies of courtroom behavior reveal that when jurors don't like a witness, they turn their feet toward the nearest exit (Dimitrius & Mazzarella, 2002, 193). From the waist up, the jurors politely face the witness who is speaking, but will turn their feet toward the natural "escape route"—such as the door leading to the hallway or the jury room.

What is true for jurors in a courtroom is also true for person-to-person interactions in general. From the hips up, we will face the person with whom we are talking. But if we are displeased with the conversation, our feet will shift away, toward the nearest exit. When a person turns his feet away, it is normally a sign of *disengagement,* a desire to distance himself from where he is currently positioned. When you are talking with someone and you note that he gradually or suddenly shifts his feet away from you, this is information you need to process. Why did the behavior take place? Sometimes it is a signal that the person is late for an appointment and really has to go; other times it is a sign that the person no longer wants to be around you. Perhaps you have said something offensive or done something annoying. The shifting foot behavior is a sign that the person wants to depart (see figure 18). However, now it is up to you—based on the circumstances surrounding the behavior—to determine *why* the individual is anxious to go (see box 15).

BOX 15: **HOW FEET WAVE GOODBYE**

When two people talk to each other, they normally speak toe to toe. If, however, one of the individuals turns his feet slightly away or repeatedly moves one foot in an outward direction (in an L formation with one foot toward you and one away from you), you can be assured he wants to take leave or wishes he were somewhere else. This type of foot behavior is another example of an intention cue (Givens, 2005, 60–61). The person's torso may remain facing you out of social diligence, but the feet may more honestly reflect the limbic brain's need or desire to escape (see figure 18).

Recently I was with a client who had spent almost five hours with me. As we were parting for the evening, we reflected on what we had covered that day. Even though our conversation was very collegial, I noticed that my client was holding one leg at a right angle to his body, seemingly wanting to take off on its own. At that point I said, "You really do have to leave now, don't you?" "Yes," he admitted. "I am so sorry. I didn't want to be rude but I have to call London and I only have five minutes!" Here was a case where my client's language and most of his body revealed nothing but positive feelings. His feet, however, were the most honest communicators, and they clearly told me that as much as he wanted to stay, duty was calling.

Fig. 18

Where one foot points and turns away during a conversation, this is a sign the person has to leave, precisely in that direction. This is an intention cue.

The Knee Clasp

There are other examples of *intention movements* of the legs that are associated with an individual who wants to leave his current location. Take note if a person who is sitting down places both hands on his knees in a knee clasp (see figure 19). This is a very clear sign that in his mind, he is ready to conclude the meeting and take leave. Usually this hands-on-knees gesture is followed by a forward lean of the torso and/or a shift of the lower body to the edge of the chair, both intention movements. When

Clasping of the knees and shifting of weight on the feet is an intention cue that the person wants to get up and leave.

you note these cues, particularly when they come from your superiors, it's time to end your interaction; be astute and don't linger.

Gravity-Defying Behaviors of the Feet

When we are happy and excited, we walk as if we are floating on air. We see this with lovers enthralled to be around each other as well as with children who are eager to enter a theme park. Gravity seems to hold no boundaries for those who are excited. These behaviors are quite obvious, and yet every day, all around us, *gravity-defying behaviors* seemingly elude our observation.

When we are excited about something or feel very positive about our circumstances, we tend to defy gravity by doing such things as rocking up and down on the balls of our feet, or walking with a bit of a bounce in our step. This is the limbic brain, once again, manifesting itself in our nonverbal behaviors.

Recently I was watching a stranger talk on his cell phone. As he listened, his left foot, which had been resting flat on the ground, changed position. The heel of the foot remained on the ground, but the rest of his shoe moved up, so that his toes were pointing skyward (see figure 20). To the average person, that behavior would have gone unnoticed or been disregarded as insignificant. But to the trained observer, that gravity-defying foot behavior can be readily decoded to mean that the man on the phone had just heard something positive. Sure enough, as I walked by I could hear him say, "Really—that's terrific!" His feet had already silently said the same thing.

Even when standing still, a person telling a story may inch up to a taller stance, elevating himself to emphasize his points, and he may do so repeatedly. The individual does this subconsciously; therefore these elevating behaviors are very honest cues, since they tend to be true expres-

Fig. 20

When the toes point upward as in this photograph, it usually means the person is in a good mood or is thinking or hearing something positive.

sions of the emotion attached to the story. They appear in real time along with the story line and relate his feelings along with his words. Just as we move our feet to the beat and tempo of a song we like, so too will we move our feet and legs in congruence with something positive we say.

Interestingly, gravity-defying behaviors of the feet and legs are rarely seen in people suffering from clinical depression. The body reflects precisely the emotional state of the individual. So when people are excited we tend to see many more gravity-defying behaviors.

Can gravity-defying behaviors be faked? I suppose they can be, particularly by really good actors and perennial liars, but average people simply don't know how to regulate their limbic behaviors. When people try to control their limbic reactions or gravity-defying behaviors, it looks contrived. Either they appear too passive or restrained for the situation or not animated enough. A faked upward arm greeting just doesn't cut it. It looks fake because the arms are not up for very long, and usually the elbows are bent. The gesture has all the hallmarks of being contrived. True gravity-defying behaviors are usually a very good barometer of a person's positive emotional state and they look genuine.

One type of gravity-defying behavior that can be very informative to the astute observer is known as the *starter's position* (see figure 21). This is an action in which a person moves his or her feet from a resting position (flat on the ground) to a ready or "starter's" position with heel elevated and weight on the balls of the feet. This is an intention cue that tells us the person is getting ready to *do* something physical, requiring foot movement. It could mean the individual intends to engage you further, is really interested, or wants to leave. As with all nonverbal intention cues, once you learn a person is about to do something, you need to rely on the context and what you know about the individual to make your best assessment of what that something is going to be.

Leg Splay

The most unmistakable and easily spotted foot and leg behaviors are *territorial displays*. Most mammals, human or not, can become territorial

When feet shift from flat footed to the
"starter's position," this is an intention cue
that the person wants to go.

when they are stressed or upset, when they are being threatened, or, conversely, when they are threatening others. In each case, they will exhibit behaviors indicating they are trying to reestablish control of their situation and their territory. Law enforcement and military personnel use these behaviors because they are accustomed to being in charge. Sometimes, they will try to outdo each other, at which point it becomes farcical as each person tries to splay out wider than his colleagues in a subconscious attempt to claim more territory.

When people find themselves in confrontational situations, their feet and legs will splay out, not only for greater balance but also to claim greater territory. This sends out a very strong message to the careful observer that at a minimum there are issues afoot or that there is potential for real trouble. When two people face off in disagreement, you will never see their legs crossed so that they are off balance. The limbic brain simply will not allow this to take place.

If you observe a person's feet going from being together to being spread apart, you can be fairly confident that the individual is becoming increasingly unhappy. This dominant stance communicates very clearly, "Something is wrong and I am ready to deal with it." Territorial leg splays signal the potential for tempers to flare; thus, whether you find yourself observing or using this type of nonverbal behavior, you should be on the alert for possible trouble.

Because people often assume a more splayed posture when an argument escalates, I tell executives as well as law enforcement officers that one way to diffuse a confrontation is to avoid using such territorial displays. If we catch ourselves in a leg-splay posture during a heated exchange and immediately bring our legs together, it often lessens the confrontation level and reduces the tension.

A few years ago, while I was conducting a seminar, a woman in the audience spoke about how her ex-husband used to intimidate her during an argument by standing in the doorway of their house, legs splayed, blocking her exit. This is not a behavior to be taken lightly. It resonates visually as well as viscerally and can be used to control, intimidate, and threaten. In fact, predators (e.g., psychopaths, antisocials) often use this leg-splay behavior in conjunction with eye-gaze behavior to control others. As one prison inmate once told me, "In here, it's all about posture, how we stand, how we look. We can't look weak, not for one moment." I suspect anywhere we might encounter predators, we should be cognizant of our posture and stance.

There are, of course, times when a leg splay can be used to your advantage—specifically, when you want to establish authority and control over others for a positive reason. I have had to coach female law enforcement officers to use the leg splay to establish a more aggressive stance when responding to unruly crowds in the line of duty. Standing with their feet together (which is perceived as submissive) sends the wrong kind of signal to a would-be antagonist. By moving their feet apart, the female officers can take a more dominant, "I am in charge" stance, which will be perceived as more authoritarian and thus help them be more effective in controlling unruly individuals. You may want to emphasize to a teenage son how you feel about smoking not by raising your voice, but rather by using a territorial display.

The Territorial Imperative

When discussing leg splay and territorial claims, we must recognize the work of Edward Hall, who studied the use of space in humans and other animals. By studying what he termed the *territorial imperative,* he was able to document our spatial needs, which he referred to as *proxemics* (Hall, 1969). Hall found that the more advantaged we are socioeconomically or hierarchically, the more territory we demand. He also found that people who tend to take up more space (territory) through their daily activities also tend to be more self-assured, more confident, and of course more likely to be of higher status. This phenomenon has been demonstrated throughout human history and in most cultures. In fact, the conquistadores witnessed it when they arrived in the new world. Once here, they saw the same territorial displays in the people native to the Americas that they had seen in Queen Isabella's court; to wit, royalty—in any country—can command and is afforded greater space (Diaz, 1988).

While CEOs, presidents, and high-status individuals can claim greater space, for the rest of us, it is not so easy. All of us, however, are very protective of our personal space, regardless of its size. We don't like it when people stand too close. In his research, Edward Hall found that each of us has a space requirement he called proxemics, that is both personal and cultural in origin. When people violate that space, we have powerful limbic reactions indicative of stress. Violations of personal space cause us to become hypervigilant; our pulse races and we may become flushed (Knapp & Hall, 2002, 146–147). Just think about how you feel when someone gets too close, whether in a crowded elevator or while you're conducting a transaction at an ATM machine. I mention these space issues so that the next time someone stands too close or you violate someone's space, you are aware of the negative limbic arousal that will take place.

Feet/Leg Displays of High Comfort

Careful observation of the legs and feet can help you determine how comfortable you are around somebody else and vice versa. *Leg crossing* is a particularly accurate barometer of how comfortable we feel around another person; we don't use it if we feel uncomfortable (see figure 22). We also cross our legs in the presence of others when we are confident—and confidence is part of comfort. Let's examine why this is such an honest and revealing lower limb behavior.

When you cross one leg in front of the other while standing, you reduce your balance significantly. From a safety standpoint, if there were a real threat, you could neither freeze very easily nor run away because, in that stance, you are basically balanced on one foot. For this reason, the limbic brain allows us to perform this behavior only when we feel comfortable or confident. If a person is standing by herself in an elevator with one leg crossed over the other, she will immediately uncross her legs and plant both feet firmly on the floor when a stranger steps into the elevator. This is a sign that the limbic brain is saying, "You can't take any chances; you may have to deal with a potential threat or problem now, so put both feet firmly on the ground!"

When I see two colleagues talking to each other and they both have their legs crossed, I know they are comfortable with each other. First,

Fig. 22

We normally cross our legs when we feel comfortable. The sudden presence of someone we don't like will cause us to uncross our legs.

this shows a *mirroring* of behaviors between two individuals (a comfort sign known as *isopraxism*) and second, because leg crossing is a high-comfort display (see figure 23). This leg-cross nonverbal can be used in interpersonal relationships to let the other person know that things are good between the two of you, so good, in fact, that you can afford to relax totally (limbically) around that individual. Leg crossing, then, becomes a great way to communicate a positive sentiment.

Recently I attended a party in Coral Gables, Florida, where I was introduced to two women, both of whom were in their early sixties. During the introduction, one of the women suddenly crossed her legs so that she

Fig. 23

When two people are talking and both have crossed their legs, this is an indication that they are very comfortable around each other.

was on one foot leaning toward her friend. I commented, "You ladies must have known each other for a long time." Their eyes and faces lit up, and one asked how I knew this. I said, "Even though you were meeting me—a stranger—for the first time, one of you crossed your legs to favor the other. That is very unusual unless you really like and trust each other." They both giggled and one inquired, "Can you read minds, too?" To which I laughed and answered, "No." After I had explained what gave their long-term friendship away, one of the two women confirmed they had known each other since they were in grade school in Cuba in the forties. Once again, the leg cross proved to be an accurate barometer of human sentiments.

Here's an interesting feature of leg crossing. We usually do it subconsciously in favor of the person we like the most. In other words, we cross our legs in such a way so that we tilt toward the person we favor. This can provide some interesting revelations during family gatherings. In families in which there are multiple children, it is not unusual to have a parent reveal a preference for one child over another by crossing legs so that they tilt toward the child they favor.

Be aware that sometimes criminals, when they are up to no good, will lean against a wall with their legs crossed when they see police driving by, pretending to be cool. Because this behavior goes counter to the threat the limbic brain is sensing, these criminals usually don't hold this behavior for very long. Experienced officers on the beat can immediately see that these subjects are posing, not reposing, but to the unknowing, they may look erroneously benign.

Feet/Leg Displays During Courtship

During high-comfort social interactions, our feet and legs will mirror those of the other person we are with (isopraxis) and will remain playful. In fact, in the extreme stages of comfort during courtship, the feet will also engage the other person through subtle foot touches or caresses (see box 16).

During courtship, and particularly while seated, a woman will often

BOX 16: **GETTING A TOEHOLD ON ROMANCE**

I was in Los Angeles this year giving nonverbal communication training to a client who works in the television industry. He was kind enough to take me to dinner at a popular Mexican restaurant near his house. While there, he wanted to continue learning about body language and pointed to a couple seated at a nearby table. He asked, "Based on what you see, do you think they're getting along with each other?" As we observed the two diners, we noted that at first they were leaning in to each other, but as the dinner and conversation progressed, they both leaned back in their chairs away from each other, not really saying much. My client thought things were going sour between them. I said, "Don't just look above the table, look under the table as well." This was easy to do, as there was no table cloth or other obstacle blocking the underside of the table. "Notice how their feet are very close to each other," I pointed out. If they weren't getting along, their feet would not be that close together. The limbic brain simply would not allow it. Now that I had him focused on the couple's feet, we noticed that every once in a while their feet touched or brushed against each other and neither person's legs retracted. "That behavior is important," I noted. "It shows they still feel connected." When the couple got up to leave, the man put his arm around the woman's waist and they walked out without saying another word. The nonverbals said it all, even though they were not in a talking mood.

If you have ever wondered why there is so much leg touching and flirting under tables or in swimming pools, it is probably related to two phenomena. First, when our body parts are out of sight, such as under a table or under water (or under the covers), they seem out of mind—or at least out of the realm of observation. We have all seen people act in a public pool as if they were in private. Second, our feet contain a tremendous number of sensory receptors, the pathways of which terminate in an area of the brain that is close to the place in which sensations of the genitalia are registered (Givens, 2005, 92–93). People play footsies under the table because it feels good and can be very sexually arousing. Conversely, when we don't like someone or don't feel close to them, we move our feet away immediately if they accidentally touch beneath the table. As a relationship wanes, a very clear sign couples often miss is that there will be progressively less foot touching of any kind.

play with her shoes and dangle them from the tips of her toes when she feels comfortable with her companion. This behavior will, however, quickly cease if the woman suddenly feels uncomfortable. A potential suitor can get a pretty good reading on how things are going based on this "shoe-play" behavior. If, upon approaching a woman (or after talking with her for a while), her shoe play stops, she adjusts her shoe back on her foot, and especially if she follows this by turning slightly away from the suitor and perhaps gathering up her purse, well, in the language of baseball, that suitor has most likely just struck out. Even when a woman is not touching her suitor with her foot, this type of foot dangling and shoe play is movement, and movement draws attention. Therefore, this nonverbal behavior says, "Notice me," which is just the opposite of the freeze response, and is part of the *orienting reflex* that is instinctive and draws us near to the things and people we like or desire and away from those things we don't like, don't trust, or of which we are not sure.

Seated leg crosses are also revealing. When people sit side by side, the direction of their leg crosses become significant. If they are on good terms, the top leg crossed over will point toward the other person. If a person *doesn't* like a topic his companion brings up, he will switch the position of the legs so that the thigh becomes a barrier (see figures 24 and 25). Such blocking behavior is another meaningful example of the limbic brain protecting us. If there is congruence in the way both parties are sitting and crossing their legs, then there is harmony.

Fig. 24

In this photo the man has placed his right leg in such a way that the knee acts as a barrier between himself and the woman.

Fig. 25

In this photo the man has positioned his leg so that the knee is further away, removing barriers between himself and the woman.

Our Need for Space

Ever wonder what kind of first impression you've made on someone? Whether they seem to like you from the outset or, rather, if there could be difficulties brewing? One way to find out is the "shake and wait" approach. Here's how it works.

Foot and leg behavior is especially important to observe when you first meet people. It reveals a lot about how they feel about you. Personally, when I first meet someone, I typically lean in, give the person a hearty handshake (depending on the appropriate cultural norms in the situation), make good eye contact, and then take a step back and see what happens next. One of three responses is likely to take place: (a) the person will remain in place, which lets me know he or she is comfortable at that distance; (b) the individual will take a step back or turn slightly away, which lets me know he or she needs more space or wants to be elsewhere; or (c) the person will actually take a step closer to me, which means he or she feels comfortable and/or favorable toward me. I take no offense to the individual's behavior because I am simply using this opportunity to see how he or she really feels about me.

Remember, the feet are the most honest part of the body. If a person needs extra space, I give it. If he or she is comfortable, I don't have to worry about dealing with a proximity issue. If someone takes a step toward me, I know they feel more comfortable near me. This is useful information in any social setting, but also remember you should set limits as to what makes *you* comfortable when it comes to space.

Walking Style

When it comes to the feet and legs, I would be remiss if I didn't mention the nonverbal cues given off by different styles of walking. According to Desmond Morris, scientists recognize approximately forty different styles of walking (Morris, 1985, 229–230). If that seems like a lot, just recall what you know about the gait of these individuals as portrayed in various films: Charlie Chaplin, John Wayne, Mae West, or Groucho Marx.

Each of these movie characters had a distinctive walking style, and their personalities were revealed, in part, through their gaits. How we walk often reflects our moods and attitudes. We can walk briskly and intentionally, or slowly in a bewildered state. We can stroll, amble, saunter, plod, waddle, limp, shuffle, prowl, bustle, march, promenade, tiptoe, swagger, and so on, to name just a few of the recognized walking styles (Morris, 1985, 233–235).

For observers of nonverbals, these walking styles are important because changes in the way people normally walk can reflect changes in their thoughts and emotions. A person who is normally happy and gregarious might suddenly change his or her walking style when told a loved one has been injured. Bad or tragic news may cause a person to sprint out of a room in desperation to help out or it may cause the individual to walk out phlegmatically as though the weight of the world is on his or her shoulders.

Changes in walking style are important nonverbal behaviors because they warn us that something might be amiss, that a problem might be lurking, that circumstances might have changed—in short, that something significant might have occurred. A change tells us that we need to assess *why* the person's gait has suddenly changed, particularly since such information can often aid us in dealing more effectively with that individual in upcoming interactions. A person's walk can help us detect things he or she is unknowingly revealing (see box 17).

Cooperative vs. Noncooperative Feet

If you are dealing with a person who is socializing or cooperative with you, his or her feet should mirror your own. If, however, someone's feet are pointed away from you while his body faces toward you, you should ask yourself why. Despite the direction of the body, this is not a genuine cooperation profile and is indicative of several things that must be explored. Such a pose reflects either the person's need to leave or get away soon, a disinterest in what is being discussed, an unwillingness to further assist, or a lack of commitment to what is being said. Note that when

---

BOX 17: **CRIME SHOPPERS**

Criminals don't always realize just how much information they give away. When I worked in New York City, my fellow agents and I often watched street predators as they tried to blend into the crowd. One of the ways in which they were unsuccessful in doing so, however, was that they frequently walked on the inside of the sidewalk, habitually changing their walking speed as they aimlessly window shopped. Most people have a place to go and a task to accomplish, so they walk with purpose. Predators (muggers, drug dealers, thieves, con men) lurk about waiting for their next victim; therefore their postures and pace are different. There is no purposeful direction to their travel until they are about to strike. When a predator vectors toward you, whether a beggar or a mugger, the discomfort you sense is due to the calculations your limbic brain is performing to try to prevent you from becoming the next target. So, next time you're in a big city, keep an eye out for predators. If you see a person walking around with no purpose who suddenly makes a beeline for you, look out! Better yet, get out—as quickly as possible. Even if you just sense this is happening, listen to your inner voice (de Becker, 1997, 133).

---

someone we don't know approaches us on the street, we usually turn our attention to them from the hips up, but keep our feet pointed in the direction of travel. The message we are sending is that socially I will be attentive briefly; personally I am prepared to continue or flee.

Over the years, I have conducted training for customs inspectors in the United States and abroad. I have learned an incredible amount from them, and I hope they have picked up a few pointers from me. One thing I have taught them is to look for passengers who point their feet toward the exit while turning to the officer to make their customs declaration (see figure 26). While they could simply be in a hurry to catch a flight, this behavior should make the inspector suspicious. In studies, we found that people who

Fig. 26

When a person talks to you with feet pointed away, it is a good indication this person wants to be elsewhere. Watch for people who make formal declarations in this position, as this is a form of distancing.

make affirmative declarations such as "I have nothing to declare, officer," but have their feet turned away are more likely to be concealing something they should have declared. In essence, their faces are obliging, their words are definitive, but their feet reveal they are being less than cooperative.

Significant Change in Intensity of Foot and/or Leg Movement

Leg twitching and movement is normal; some people do it all the time, others never. It is not indicative of lying—as some erroneously believe—as both honest and dishonest people will twitch and jiggle. The key factor to consider is at what point do these behaviors start or change. For instance, years ago Barbara Walters was interviewing Academy Awards nominee Kim Basinger prior to the awards ceremony. Throughout the interview, Ms. Basinger jiggled her feet and her hands seemed to be very nervous. When Ms. Walters began to ask Ms. Basinger about some financial difficulties and a questionable investment she and her then husband had made, Ms. Basinger's foot went from jiggling to kicking. It was instantaneous and remarkable. Again, this does not mean she was lying or even intended to lie in response to the question, but it was clearly a visceral reaction to a negative stimulus (the question asked) and it reflected her disdain for the inquiry.

Anytime there is a shift from foot jiggling to foot kicking in a seated person, according to Dr. Joe Kulis, it is a very good indicator that the person has seen or heard something negative and is not happy about it (see figure 27). While jiggling may be a show of nervousness, kicking is a subconscious way of combating the unpleasant. The beauty of this behavior is that it is automatic, and most people don't even recognize they are doing it. You can use this nonverbal body signal to your advantage by creating questions that will evince the *leg-kick response* (or any other dramatic change in nonverbals) to determine what specific inquiries or

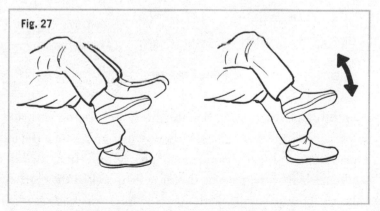

Fig. 27

When a foot suddenly begins to kick, it is usually a good indicator of discomfort. You see this with people being interviewed, as soon as a question is asked they do not like.

subjects are problematic. In this manner, even hidden facts may be elicited from people, whether they answer the question or not (see box 18).

BOX 18: **FORGET BONNIE, FIND CLYDE**

I vividly recall an interview I conducted with a woman who was thought to be a witness to a serious crime. For hours the interview session was going nowhere; it was frustrating and tedious. The interviewee revealed no significant behaviors; however, I did notice she jiggled her foot all the time. Because it was a relative constant, this behavior was of no consequence until I asked the question, "Do you know Clyde?" Immediately upon hearing that question, and even though she didn't answer (at least not verbally), the woman's foot went from jiggling to an elevated up-and-down kicking motion. This was a significant clue that this name had a negative effect on her. In further questioning, she later admitted that "Clyde" had involved her in stealing government documents from a base in Germany. Her leg-kick reaction was a significant clue to us that there was something more to explore, and in the end her confession proved that suspicion to be accurate. Ironically, that betraying behavior probably made her want to kick herself, because it ultimately cost her twenty-five years in a federal prison.

Foot Freeze

If a person constantly wiggles or bounces his or her feet or leg(s) and suddenly stops, you need to take notice. This usually signifies that the individual is experiencing stress, an emotional change, or feels threatened in some way. Ask yourself why the person's limbic system kicked their survival instincts into the "freeze" mode. Perhaps something was said or asked that might lead to revealing information the person doesn't want you to know. Possibly the individual has done something and is afraid you will find him out. The *foot freeze* is another example of a limbic-controlled response, the tendency of an individual to stop activity when faced with danger.

The Foot Lock and Leave

When an individual suddenly turns his toes inward or interlocks his feet, it is a sign that he is insecure, anxious, and/or feels threatened. When interviewing suspects in crimes, I often notice that they interlock their feet and ankles when they are under stress. A lot of people, especially women, have been taught to sit this way, especially when wearing a skirt (see figure 28). However, to lock the ankles in this way, especially over a prolonged period, is unnatural and should be considered suspect, particularly when done by males.

Fig. 28

A sudden interlocking of the legs may suggest discomfort or insecurity. When people are comfortable, they tend to unlock their ankles.

Interlocking ankles is again part of the limbic response to freeze in the face of a threat. Experienced nonverbal observers have noted how often people who are lying will not move their feet in an interview, seeming frozen, or they interlock their feet in such a way as to restrict movement. This is consistent with research indicating that people tend to restrict arm and leg movements when lying (Vrij, 2003, 24–27). Having said this, I want to caution you that lack of movement is not in itself indicative of deception; it is indicative of self-restraint and caution, which both nervous and lying individuals utilize to assuage their concerns.

Some individuals take the interlocking feet or ankles one step further; they actually lock their feet around the legs of their chair (see figure 29). This is a *restraining* (freeze) *behavior* that tells us, once again, that something is troubling the person (see box 19).

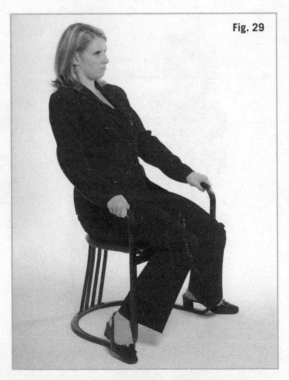

Fig. 29

The sudden locking of ankles around the legs of a chair is part of the freeze response and is indicative of discomfort, anxiety, or concern.

BOX 19: **MAKE THAT A DOUBLE FREEZE**

You should always be on the lookout for multiple tells (tell clusters) that point to the same behavioral conclusion. They strengthen the likelihood that your conclusion is correct. In the case of the foot lock, watch for the individual who locks his feet around his chair legs and then moves his hand along his pants leg (as if drying his hand on his trousers). The foot lock is a freeze response and the leg rubbing is a pacifying behavior. The two, taken together, make it more likely that the person has been uncovered; he fears something he has done will be found out and he is experiencing stress because of this.

Sometimes a person will signal stress by attempting to hide the feet altogether. When you are speaking with someone, watch to see if that individual moves his or her feet from in front of the chair to under the chair. There is no scientific research (yet) to document what I am about to say. However, over the years, I have observed that when a high-stress question is asked, the respondent will often withdraw his or her feet beneath the chair, which could be seen as a distancing reaction and one that attempts to minimize the exposed parts of the body. This cue can be used to evince discomfort about particular issues and help channel the investigative inquiry. As the observer watches, the interviewee—through his feet and legs—will tell you those things about which he does not wish to talk. As the subject changes and becomes less stressful, the feet will emerge again, expressing the limbic brain's relief that the stressful topic is no longer being discussed.

SUMMING IT UP

Because they have been so directly critical to our survival throughout human evolution, our feet and legs are the most honest parts of the body.

Our lower limbs provide the most accurate, uncensored information to the alert observer. Used skillfully, this information can help you get a better read on others in all manner of settings. When you combine your knowledge of foot and leg nonverbals with signals from other parts of the body, you become even more capable of understanding what people are thinking, feeling, and intending to do. Therefore, let's turn our attention to those other parts of the body now. Next stop, the human torso.

FOUR

Torso Tips

Nonverbals of the Torso, Hips, Chest, and Shoulders

This chapter will cover the hips, abdomen, chest, and shoulders, collectively known as the *torso*, or *trunk*. As with the legs and feet, many of the behaviors associated with the torso reflect the true sentiments of the emotional (limbic) brain. Because the torso houses many vital internal organs, such as the heart, lungs, liver, and digestive tract, we can anticipate that the brain will seek to diligently protect this area when threatened or challenged. During times of danger, whether real or perceived, the brain recruits the rest of the body to guard these crucial organs in ways that range from the subtle to the more obvious. Let's look at some of the more common nonverbal signals of the torso and some examples of how these behaviors project what is going on in the brain—particularly the limbic brain.

SIGNIFICANT NONVERBAL BEHAVIORS INVOLVING THE TORSO, HIPS, CHEST, AND SHOULDERS

The Torso Lean

Like much of our body, the torso will react to perceived dangers by attempting to distance itself from anything stressful or unwanted. For instance, when an object is thrown at us, our limbic system sends signals to the torso to move away instantly from that threat. Typically this will happen regardless of the nature of the object; if we sense movement in our direction, we will pull away, whether from a baseball or a moving car.

In a similar fashion, when an individual is standing next to someone who is being obnoxious or someone he does not like, his torso will lean away from that individual (see box 20). Because the torso carries a large portion of our weight and transmits it to the lower limbs, any reorientation of our trunks requires energy and balance. Therefore, when one's torso does lean away from something, it is because the brain demands it; so we can count on the honesty of these reactions. Extra effort and energy are required to hold these positions. Just try to maintain any off-center position consciously, whether bowing down or leaning away, and you will find that your body soon tires. However, when such off-balance behavior is performed because your brain subconsciously decides it's a necessity, you will hardly feel it or notice it.

Not only do we lean away from people who make us uncomfortable, we may also blade away (turn slightly) by degrees from that which does not appeal to us or we grow to dislike. Not long after it opened, I took my daughter to the Holocaust Museum in Washington, D.C., which is something every visitor to D.C. should do. As we walked around the memorable exhibits, I noticed how young and old first approached each exhibit. Some walked right up, leaning into it while trying to absorb every nuance. Some approached hesitantly, while others would draw near, then begin to turn slowly and slightly away as the inhumanity of the Nazi regime encroached on their senses. Some, stunned by the depravity they were witnessing, turned 180 degrees and faced the other way, as

---

BOX 20: **WILY OR WEIRD?**

Years ago I was stationed in the New York office of the FBI. During my tenure there, I had numerous opportunities to ride the trains and subways in and out of the city. It didn't take long to recognize the many different techniques people used to claim territory while on public transport. It seemed there was always someone who sat on the seat but whose body would sway from side to side so as to impose on others or whose arms would flail wildly at times while holding one of the straps. These individuals always seemed to possess more space around them because no one wanted to get near them. When forced to sit or stand next to these "weirdos," people would lean at the torso as far as possible so as not to come in contact with them. You have to ride the subways in New York to appreciate this. I am convinced that some passengers purposely acted strangely and exaggerated their body movements to keep people at a distance, away from their torsos. In fact, a long-time resident of New York once told me, "If you want to keep the hordes at bay, act like you're nuts!" Perhaps he was right.

---

they waited for their friends to finish examining the display. Their brains were saying, "I can't handle this," and so their bodies turned away. The human species has evolved to the point that not only physical proximity to a person we dislike can cause us to lean away, but even images of unpleasant things, such as photographs, can cause a torso lean.

As a careful observer of human behavior, you need to be aware that distancing sometimes takes place abruptly or very subtly; a mere shifting of body angle of just a few degrees is enough to express negative sentiment. For example, couples who are pulling apart emotionally will also begin to pull apart physically. Their hands don't touch as much, and their torsos actually avoid each other. When they sit side by side, they will lean away from each other. They create a silent space between them, and when they are forced to sit next to each other, such as in the back of an automobile, they will only rotate toward each other with their heads, not their bodies.

Ventral Denial and Ventral Fronting

These torso displays that reflect the limbic brain's need to distance and avoid are very good indicators of true sentiments. When one person in a relationship feels that something is wrong with the way things are going, he or she is most likely sensing a subtle degree of physical distancing in his or her partner. The distancing can also take the form of what I call *ventral denial*. Our ventral (front) side, where our eyes, mouth, chest, breasts, genitals, etc. are located, is very sensitive to things we like and dislike. When things are good, we expose our ventral sides toward what we favor, including those people who make us feel good. When things go wrong, relationships change, or even when topics are discussed that we disfavor, we will engage in ventral denial, by shifting or turning away. The ventral side is the most vulnerable side of the body, so the limbic brain has an inherent need to protect it from the things that hurt or bother us. This is the reason, for example, we immediately and subconsciously begin to turn slightly to the side when someone we dislike approaches us at a party. When it comes to courtship, an increase in ventral denial is one of the best indicators that the relationship is in trouble.

In addition to visual input, the limbic brain can also have a reaction to conversations we find distasteful. Watch any TV talk show with the volume off and notice how the guests will lean away from each other as they present contrary arguments. Not long ago, I was watching the Republican presidential debates and noted that even though the candidates were spaced quite far apart, they still leaned away from each other when issues were brought up with which they disagreed.

The opposite of ventral denial is ventral exposure or—as I like to call it—*ventral fronting*. We display our ventral sides to those we favor. When our children come running to us for a hug, we move objects, even our arms, out of the way so that we can give them access to our ventral sides. We ventrally front because this is where we feel the most warmth and comfort. In fact, we use the phrase *turning our back* to express negativity toward someone or something, because we offer our ventral sides to those we care for and our backs to those we don't.

Similarly, we demonstrate comfort by using our torsos and shoulders to lean in the direction of that which we favor. In a classroom, it's not unusual to see students leaning toward a favorite teacher without realizing they are bent forward, almost out of their chairs, hanging on every word. Remember the scene from the movie *Raiders of the Lost Ark* when the students were leaning forward to hear their professor? Their nonverbal behavior clearly indicated they admired him.

Lovers can be seen leaning across a café table, their faces coming close to each other to gain more intimate visual contact. They front their ventral selves toward each other, exposing their most vulnerable parts. This is a natural, evolutionary response of the limbic brain that has social benefit. By moving closer together and exposing our ventral (weakest) side when we like someone or something, we show that we are giving ourselves in an unrestrained manner. Reciprocating this positioning by mirroring, or isopraxism, demonstrates social harmony by rewarding the intimacy and showing it is appreciated.

Nonverbal limbic behaviors of the torso, such as leaning, distancing, and ventral exposure or denial, happen all the time in boardrooms and other meetings. Colleagues who share a similar point of view will sit closer together, turn more toward each other ventrally, and will lean harmoniously nearer each other. When people disagree, they will hold their bodies firm, avoid ventral fronting (unless challenged), and will most likely lean away from each other (see figures 30 and 31). This behavior subconsciously tells others, "I am not in agreement with your idea." As with all nonverbals, these actions need to be analyzed in context. For example, people new to a job may seem stiff and inflexible at a meeting. Rather than reflecting dislike or disagreement, this rigid posture and limited arm activity may simply indicate that they are nervous in a new environment.

Not only can we use this information to read the body language of others, but we must also always remember that we are projecting our own nonverbals. During conversations or meetings, as information and opinions flow, our feelings about the news and viewpoints also will flow and be reflected in our ever-changing nonverbal behaviors. If we hear

Fig. 30

People lean toward each other when there is high comfort and agreement. This mirroring or isopraxis starts when we are babies.

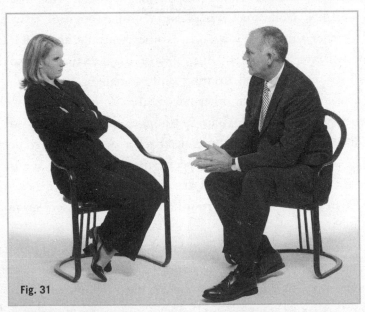

Fig. 31

We lean away from things and people we don't like, even from colleagues when they say things with which we don't agree.

something distasteful one minute and something favorable the next, our bodies will reflect this shift in our feelings.

A very powerful way to let others know that you agree with them, or are consciously contemplating what they are saying, is to lean toward them or to ventrally front them. This tactic is especially effective when you are in a meeting and you don't have the opportunity to speak up.

The Torso Shield

When it is impractical or socially unacceptable to lean away from someone or something we dislike, we often subconsciously use our arms or objects to act as barriers (see figure 32). Clothing or nearby objects

Fig. 32

A sudden crossing of the arms during a conversation could indicate discomfort.

BOX 21: PILLOW TALK

When we see individuals suddenly protecting their torsos, we can assume they are not comfortable and that they sense themselves to be in some kind of threatening or dangerous situation. In 1992, while working with the FBI, I interviewed a young man and his father in a hotel room in the Boston area. The father had agreed, reluctantly, to bring the young man to the interview. While sitting on the hotel couch, the young man grabbed one of the couch pillows and held it close to his chest for most of the three-hour interview. Despite the presence of his father, this young man felt vulnerable and, therefore, needed to tightly clutch a "security blanket." While the barrier was only a pillow, it must have been quite effective for this individual, because there was just no getting through to him. I found it remarkable that when the subject was neutral, such as when we talked about his involvement in sports, he would put the pillow aside. However, when we spoke of his possible complicity in a major crime, he would retrieve the pillow and press it tightly against his torso. It was clear that the only time his limbic brain felt the need to protect his torso was when he felt threatened. He never did reveal anything at this meeting, but the next time he was interviewed, the comforting pillows were conspicuously absent!

(see box 21) also serve the same purpose. For instance, a businessmen may suddenly decide to button his jacket when talking to someone with whom he is uncomfortable, only to undo the jacket as soon as the conversation is over.

Buttoning a jacket, of course, is not always an indication of discomfort; often men will button their jackets to formalize a setting or to show deference to their boss. It is *not* the kind of total comfort we might find at, say, a barbecue, but neither does it indicate uneasiness. Clothing and how we attend to our clothes can influence perceptions and are even suggestive of how approachable or open we are to others (Knapp & Hall, 2002, 206–214).

It has always been my impression that presidents often go to Camp David to accomplish in polo shirts what they can't seem to accomplish in business suits forty miles away at the White House. By unveiling themselves ventrally (with the removal of coats) they are saying, "I am open to you." Presidential candidates send this same nonverbal message at rallies when they get rid of their jackets (their shields, if you will) and roll up their shirtsleeves in front of the "common folk."

Perhaps not surprisingly, women tend to cover their torsos even more so than men, especially when they feel insecure, nervous, or cautious. A woman may cross her arms over her stomach, just under the breasts, in an effort to shield her torso and comfort herself. She may cross one arm across her front and grab the opposite arm at the elbow, forming a barrier to her chest. Both behaviors subconsciously serve to protect and insulate, especially in social situations where there is some discomfort.

On campus, I often see women place their notebooks across their chests as they walk into class, particularly for the first few days. As their comfort level increases, they will shift to carrying their notebooks at their sides. On test days, this *chest-shielding* behavior tends to increase, even among male students. Women will also use backpacks, briefcases, or purses to shield themselves, especially when sitting alone. Just as you may pull a comforter on while watching television, putting something across the ventral torso protects and soothes us. Objects we draw toward us, especially ventrally, are usually placed there to provide the comfort we need at that moment, whatever the situation. When you witness people protecting their torsos in real time, you can use it as an accurate indicator of discomfort on their parts. By carefully assessing the circumstances, the source of that discomfort may allow you to help them or at least better understand them.

Men, for whatever the reason (perhaps to be less conspicuous), will shield their torsos, but in more subtle ways. A male may reach across the front of himself to play with his watch, or, as Prince Charles of England often does when he is in public, reach over and adjust his shirtsleeve or play with his cuff links. A man may also fix his tie knot, perhaps longer than usual, as this allows for the arm to cover the ventral area of the chest and neck. These are forms of shielding that transmit that the person is slightly insecure at that moment.

I was in a supermarket checkout line waiting for the woman in front of me to conclude her transaction. She was evidently using a debit card, and the machine kept rejecting it. Each time she swiped the card and entered her pin number, she would await the machine's response with her arms crossed across her chest, until finally she gave up and walked away, exasperated. Each time the card was rejected, her arms and grip got tighter, a clear sign that her annoyance and discomfort were escalating (see figures 33 and 34).

Children can be seen to cross or lock their arms across their bodies when upset or being defiant, even at an early age. These shielding behaviors come in a variety of forms—from arms crisscrossed over the belly to crossing the arms high with hands grasping opposite shoulders.

Students often ask me if it means there is something wrong with them if they sit in class and cross their arms in front of themselves. The question is not whether something is wrong, nor does this posture mean they are blocking the teacher out; arms intertwined across the front is a

Fig. 33

In public, many of us comfortably cross our arms while waiting or listening to a speaker. Around the house we rarely sit this way unless something is bothering us, like waiting for a late ride.

Fig. 34

Crossed arms with hands tightly gripping the arms is definitely an indication of discomfort.

very comfortable pose for many people. However, when a person suddenly crosses arms and then interlocks them tightly, with a tight hand grip, this is indicative of discomfort. Remember, it is by gauging changes from baseline postures that we can note when uneasiness arises. Watch to see if the person opens up ventrally as they become more relaxed. I find that when I give lectures, many of the participants initially will sit with their arms crossed, and then loosen them over time. Obviously, something happens to elicit this behavior; probably greater comfort with their surroundings and their instructor.

It could be argued that women (or men) cross their arms simply because they are cold. But this does not negate the nonverbal meaning, since cold is a form of discomfort. People who are uncomfortable while being interviewed (e.g., suspects in criminal investigations, children in trouble with their parents, or an employee being questioned for improper conduct) often complain of feeling cold during the interview. Regardless of the reason, when we are distressed the limbic brain engages various systems of the body in preparation for the freeze/flight-or-fight survival response. One of the effects is that blood is channeled toward the large muscles of the limbs and away from the skin, in case those muscles will need to be used to escape or combat the threat. As blood is diverted to these vital areas, some people lose their normal skin tone and will actually look pale or as if they are in shock. Since blood is the main source of our body warmth, diverting blood away from the skin and into deeper muscles makes the body's surface feel cooler (see box 22) (LeDoux, 1996, 131–133). For example, in the interview mentioned earlier in which the young man clutched the pillow, he complained of being cold the whole time we were there, even though I turned the air conditioner off. Both his father and I were fine; he was the only one complaining about the temperature.

The Torso Bow

Bowing at the waist is performed almost universally as a sign of subservience, respect, or humility when feeling honored, such as with applause. Notice, for example, how the Japanese and, to a lesser extent in modern

---

BOX 22: **WHY YOU CAN'T STOMACH CERTAIN TOPICS**

Did you ever wonder why you get an upset stomach if there is an argument at the dinner table? When you are upset, your digestive system no longer has as much blood as it needs for proper digestion. Just as your limbic system's freeze, flight, or fight response shunts blood away from the skin, it likewise diverts blood from your digestive system, sending blood to your heart and limb muscles (especially the legs) to prepare for your escape. The upset stomach you feel is a symptom of that limbic arousal. The next time an argument ensues during a meal, you will recognize the limbic response of distress. A child whose parents fight at the dinner table really can't finish his meal; his limbic system has trumped alimentation and digestion to prepare them for escape and survival. Along these lines, it is interesting to note how many people vomit after experiencing a traumatic event. In essence, during emergencies the body is saying that there is no time for digestion; the reaction is to lighten the load and prepare for escape or physical conflict (Grossman, 1996, 67–73).

---

times, the Chinese, bow out of respect and deference. We show that we are subservient or of lower status when we automatically assume a bowed or *kowtow* position, achieved principally by bending the torso.

For Westerners, kowtowing does not come easily, especially when it is a conscious act. However, as we expand our horizons and interact with more and more people from various countries of the Near East and Far East, it behooves us to learn to bow our torsos slightly, particularly when meeting those who are elderly and have earned respect. This simple gesture of reverence will be recognized by those whose cultures show deference by such posture and will confer a social advantage upon those Westerners willing to demonstrate it (see box 23). Incidentally, eastern Europeans, especially older ones, still like to click their heels and bow slightly out of respect. Every time I see this, I think how charming it is

---

BOX 23: **A SUPREME KOWTOW**

The universality of torso bows was dramatically illustrated to me in an old newsreel of General Douglas MacArthur while he was assigned to the Philippine government before World War II broke out. It shows a U.S. Army officer exiting MacArthur's office after dropping off some documents. As he leaves, the officer kowtows on his way out, backing out of the room. No one asked him to do it; the behavior was automatically prompted by the officer's brain to let the higher-status person know that his position was clear—it was a recognition that MacArthur was in charge. (Gorillas, dogs, wolves, and other nonhuman animals also demonstrate this subservient posturing.) Remarkably, the officer bowing out of the room was none other than the man who one day would become the Supreme allied commander of Europe, architect of the Normandy invasion, and our thirty-fourth president: Dwight David Eisenhower. Incidentally, years later, upon learning that Eisenhower was running for president, MacArthur commented that Eisenhower was the "finest clerk" he'd ever had (Manchester, 1978, 166).

---

that people still show graciousness and deference in today's world. Whether done consciously or subconsciously, the torso bow is a nonverbal gesture of regard for others.

Torso Embellishments

Because nonverbal communication also includes symbols, we have to give some attention to clothing and other accoutrements that are worn on the torso (including the body, in general). It is said that clothing makes the man, and I would agree, at least in terms of appearances. Numerous studies have established that what we wear, whether a suit or casual clothes—even the colors of our outfits, a blue suit as opposed to a brown suit—will influence others (Knapp & Hall, 2002, 206–214).

Clothing says a lot about us and can do a lot for us. In a sense, our torsos are billboards upon which we advertise our sentiments. During courtship, we dress up to enchant; while working we dress for success. Similarly, the high school letter jacket, the police badge, and the military decoration are all worn on the torso as a way of calling attention to our achievements. If we want others to notice us, the torso is where it's at. When the president gives his State of the Union address before Congress, the red-garbed women you notice in a sea of blue and gray are those who, like birds displaying their plumage, are wearing vibrant colors to be noticed.

Clothing can be very subdued, very sinister (consider "skinhead" attire or a "gothic" look), or very flamboyant (such as that of musicians Liberace or Elton John), reflecting the mood and/or personality of the wearer. We alternatively can use torso adornments or bare parts of our torsos to attract others, to show off how muscular or fit we are, or to advertise where we fit in socially, economically, or occupationally. This may explain why so many people fret excessively about what to wear when attending a high-profile function or going on a date. Our personal adornments allow us to show our pedigree or our allegiance to a particular group—for example, wearing the colors of our favorite team.

Clothing can be very descriptive, such as revealing when people are celebrating or mourning, if they are of high or low status, whether they conform to social norms or are part of a sect (e.g., Hasidic Jew, Amish farmer, or Hare Krishna). In a way, we are what we wear (see box 24). For years people told me I dressed like an FBI agent, and they were right. I wore the standard agent uniform: navy blue suit, white shirt, burgundy tie, black shoes, and short hair.

Obviously, because we have certain employment roles that require specific attire and since we make conscious choices when it comes to clothing, we need to be careful in our assessment of what it signifies. After all, the guy standing outside your door dressed in a telephone repairman's uniform just might be a criminal who purchased or stole the outfit to gain access to your home (see box 25 on page 100).

Even with the caveats just mentioned, clothing needs to be considered

BOX 24: YOU ARE WHAT YOU WEAR

Imagine this scenario. You are walking down a sparsely populated street one evening and you hear someone coming up behind you. You can't see the person's face or hands clearly in the dark, but you can determine he is wearing a suit and tie and carrying a briefcase. Now, imagine the same dark sidewalk, but this time picture that all you can see behind you is the outline of a person wearing disheveled and baggy clothing, sagging pants, a tilted cap, a stained T-shirt, and tennis shoes that are worn and raggedy. In either case, you can't see the person well enough to discern any other details—and you are assuming it is a man, based simply on the clothing. But based on the attire alone, you will likely draw different con-clusions about the potential threat each person poses to your safety. Even if the approaching pace of each man is the same, as the person nears, your limbic brain will activate, even though your reaction to these individ-uals will be based exclusively on your reaction to their clothing. Your assess-ment of the situation will either make you feel comfortable or uncomfortable, even potentially frightened.

I am not going to tell you which person would make *you* feel more comfortable; that is for you to decide. But right or wrong, all other things being equal, it is their clothing that often greatly influences what we think of individuals. Although clothing, itself, cannot hurt us physically, it can affect us socially. Consider how judgmental and suspicious some Ameri-cans have become since September 11, 2001, when they see a person in clothing that reflects a Middle Eastern background. And furthermore, imagine how some Middle Eastern Americans have been made to feel as a result.

I tell college students that life is not always fair and that, unfortu-nately, they will be judged by their attire; therefore they need to think carefully about their clothing choices and the messages they are sending to others.

BOX 25: WE AREN'T ALWAYS WHO WE APPEAR TO BE

Clearly, we have to be careful when we assess a person on the basis of clothing only, as it can sometimes lead to the wrong conclusion. I was in London last year at a very nice hotel just four blocks from Buckingham Palace where all of the staff, including the maids, wore Armani suits. If I had seen them on the train going to work, I could easily have been misled as to their relative social status. So remember, because it is culturally prescribed and easily manipulated, clothing is only part of the nonverbal picture. We assess clothing to determine whether it is sending a message, not to judge people based on their attire.

---

in the overall scheme of nonverbal assessment. For that reason, it is important that we wear clothes that are congruent with the messages we want to send others, assuming we want to influence their behavior in a way that is positive or beneficial to us.

When choosing your wardrobe and accessories, always remain cognizant of the message you are sending with your clothing and the meaning that others may perceive from your dress. Also consider that although you may deliberately want to use your attire to send a signal to one person or group of people at a specific time and place, you may have to pass a lot of other people who are not as receptive to your message along the way!

At seminars I frequently ask the question, "How many of you were dressed by your mother today?" Of course everyone laughs, and *no one* raises his hand. Then I say, "Well, then, you—all of you—chose to dress the way you did." That is when they all look around them and, perhaps for the first time, realize that they could do a better job of dressing and presenting themselves. After all, before two people first meet, the only input each has to go on about the other is physical appearance and other nonverbal communications. Perhaps it's time to consider how *you* are being perceived.

Preening

When we are physically and mentally well, we take care of our appearance, preening and grooming ourselves accordingly. Humans are not unique in this regard, as birds and mammals engage in like behaviors. When we are physically or mentally ill, on the other hand, the posture of the torso and shoulders, as well as our overall appearance, may signal our poor health (American Psychiatric Association, 2000, 304–307, 350–352). Many unfortunate homeless people are afflicted with schizophrenia and rarely do they attend to their attire. Their clothes are soiled and grimy, and many of these individuals will even fight attempts by others to get them to bathe or wear clean clothing. The mentally depressed person will stoop as he walks or stands, the weight of the world seemingly bringing him down.

The phenomenon of poor grooming during illness and sadness has been noted around the world by anthropologists, social workers, and health-care providers. When the brain is saddened or we are ill, preening and presentation are among the first things to go (Darwin 1872, chap. 3, passim). For example, patients recovering from surgery may walk down the hospital hallway with hair disheveled and in gowns with their backsides exposed, not caring about personal appearance. When you are really ill, you may lie around the house looking more unkempt than you ever would be normally. When a person is really sick or really traumatized, the brain has other priorities, and preening is simply not one of them. Therefore, within context, we can use an overall lack of personal hygiene and/or grooming to make assumptions about a person's state of mind or state of health.

Torso Splays

Splaying out on a couch or a chair is normally a sign of comfort. However, when there are serious issues to be discussed, splaying out is a territorial or dominance display (see figure 35). Teenagers, in particular, often will sit splayed out on a chair or bench, as a nonverbal way of dominating their environment while being chastised by their parents. This *splay behavior* is disrespectful and shows indifference to those in authority. It is a territorial display that should *not* be encouraged or tolerated.

If you have a child who does this every time he or she is in serious trouble, you need to neutralize this behavior immediately by asking your child to sit up and, if that fails, by nonverbally violating his or her space (by sitting next to or standing closely behind him or her). In short order, your child will have a limbic response to your spatial "invasion," which will cause him or her to sit up. If you allow your child to get away with torso splays during major disagreements, don't be surprised if he or she loses respect for you over time. And why not? By allowing such displays, you are basically saying, "It's OK to disrespect me." When these kids grow up, they may continue to splay out inappropriately in the workplace when they should be sitting up attentively. This is not conducive to lon-

Fig. 35

Splaying out is a territorial display, which is OK in your own home but not in the work place, especially during a job interview.

gevity on the job, since it sends a strong negative nonverbal message of disrespect for authority.

Puffing Up the Chest

Humans, like many other creatures (including some lizards, birds, dogs, and our fellow primates), puff up their chests when trying to establish territorial dominance (Givens, 1998–2007). Watch two people who are angry with each other; they will puff out their chests just like silverback gorillas. Although it may seem almost comical when we see others do it, puffing of the chest should not be ignored, because observation has shown that when people are about to strike someone their chests will puff out. You see this on the school grounds when kids are about to fight. It can also be seen among professional boxers as they goad each other verbally before a major fight—chest out, leaning into each other, proclaiming their certitude of winning. The great Muhammad Ali did this better than anyone during prefight events. Not only was he threatening he was also funny—all part of the show—which made for good theater and, of course, ticket sales.

Baring the Torso

Sometimes in street fights, people getting ready to strike out at an opponent will disrobe—removing an article of clothing like a shirt or hat. Whether this is done simply to flex one's muscles, to protect the discarded clothing, or to rob the opponent of some type of hold he can use to his advantage, no one is sure. In any case, if you should get into an argument with someone and he or she takes off a hat, shirt, or other article of clothing, most likely a fight is in the offing (see box 26).

Breathing Behavior and the Torso

When a person is under stress, the chest may be seen to heave or expand and contract rapidly. When the limbic system is aroused and engaged for

---

**BOX 26: ONE TIME YOU DON'T WANT THE
SHIRT OFF HIS BACK**

Years ago I witnessed two neighbors verbally sparring over a sprinkler system that had accidentally sprayed a freshly waxed vehicle. As things escalated, one of the neighbors started unbuttoning his shirt. It was then that I knew fists were going to fly. Sure enough, the shirt came off and the chest bumping began between them. This was a mere precursor to the punching, which soon followed. It seemed incredible that grown men would fight over water spots on a car. What was really remarkable, however, was the chest bumping between the two guys, as though they were gorillas. It was actually embarrassing to watch them engage in such a ludicrous torso display. It's just something that shouldn't happen.

---

flight or fight, the body attempts to take in as much oxygen as possible, either by breathing more deeply or by panting. The stressed individual's chest is heaving because the limbic brain is saying, "Potential problem— step up oxygen consumption in case we suddenly have to escape or fight!" When you see this type of nonverbal behavior in an otherwise healthy person, you should consider why he or she is so stressed.

Shoulder Shrugs

Full and slight shoulder shrugs can mean a lot in context. When the boss asks an employee, "Do you know anything about this customer's complaint?" and the employee answers, "No," while giving a half shrug, chances are the speaker is not committed to what was just said. An honest and true response will cause both shoulders to rise sharply and equally. Expect people to give full (high) shoulder shrugs when they confidently support what they are saying. There is nothing wrong with saying, "I don't know!" while both shoulders rise up toward the ear. As discussed previously, this is a gravity-defying behavior that normally signifies the

Partial shoulder shrugs indicate lack of commitment or insecurity.

We use shoulder shrugs to indicate lack of knowledge or doubt. Look for both shoulders to rise; when only one side rises, the message is dubious.

person is comfortable and confident with his or her actions. If you see a person's shoulders only partially rise or if only one shoulder rises, chances are the individual is not limbically committed to what he or she is saying and is probably being evasive or even deceptive (see figures 36 and 37).

Weak Shoulder Displays

Speaking of shoulders, be aware of the person who, while conversing or in reaction to a negative event, moves his or her body so the shoulders begin to slowly rise toward the ears in a manner that makes the neck seem to disappear (see figure 38). The key action here is that the shoulders rise slowly. The person displaying this body language is basically trying to make his head disappear, like a turtle. Such an individual is lacking confidence and is highly uncomfortable. I have seen this behavior in business meetings when the boss comes in and says, "OK, I want to hear what everyone has been doing." As different people around the room proudly talk about their accomplishments, the marginal employees

Fig. 38

Shoulders rising toward the ears causes
the "turtle effect"; weakness, insecurity,
and negative emotions are the message.
Think of losing athletes walking back to
the locker room.

will seemingly sink lower and lower, their shoulders rising higher and
higher in a subconscious attempt to hide their heads.

This turtlelike behavior also shows up in families when the father
says, "It really hurt my feelings to find that someone broke my reading
lamp without telling me." As the father looks at each of his children, one
will be looking down, shoulders rising toward the ears. You will also see
these weak shoulder displays demonstrated by a losing football team as
they walk back to the locker-room—their shoulders seeming to swallow
up their heads.

ONE FINAL COMMENT ON THE TORSO AND SHOULDERS

There are a lot of books on nonverbal behavior that neglect to mention the torso and the shoulders. That is unfortunate, because a lot of valuable information comes to us from this portion of our physique. If you have neglected to observe this area of the body for nonverbal clues, I hope the material in this chapter has convinced you to expand your observational range to include the "billboard" of the body. Its reactions are particularly honest because, with so many of our vital organs housed there, the limbic brain takes great care to protect our torsos.

FIVE

Knowledge Within Reach

Nonverbals of the Arms

In terms of observing body language, the arms are largely underappreciated. We typically place much more emphasis on the face and hands when seeking to read nonverbal behavior. In observing for signs of comfort, discomfort, confidence, or other displays of feeling, the arms serve well as emotive transmitters.

Since the time our primate ancestors began to walk upright, human arms were free to be used in remarkable ways. Our arms are able to carry loads, cast blows, grasp objects, and lift us off the ground. They are streamlined, agile, and provide a formidable first response to any outside threat, especially when used in conjunction with the lower limbs. If someone throws an object at us, our arms rise to block it, instinctively and accurately. Our arms, like our feet and legs, are so reactive and so oriented to protect us that they will rise up to defend us even when doing so is illogical or ill-advised. In my work in the FBI, I have seen individuals shot in the arm as they used their upper limbs in an attempt to defend themselves from handgun fire. The thinking brain would realize that an arm simply cannot stop a bullet, yet the limbic brain will cause our arms to lift and precisely block a projectile traveling at 900 feet per second. In forensic science, such injuries are known as *defense wounds*.

Every time you bump your arm—especially if you run into something sharp—consider that it may have just protected your torso from a potentially lethal blow. Once, while holding an umbrella above my head during a Florida rainstorm, the sharp edge of my car door swung back on me and struck me in the side, breaking a rib that was left unprotected by my upraised arm. Since that time, I have a painful memory that reminds me to appreciate my arms and how they protect me.

Because our arms—like our feet—are designed to assist with our survival, they can be counted upon to reveal true sentiments or intentions. Therefore, unlike the more variable and deceptive face, the upper limbs provide solid nonverbal cues that more accurately portray what we—and those around us—are thinking, feeling, or intending. In this chapter we will examine the interpretation of some of the most common arm displays.

SIGNIFICANT NONVERBAL BEHAVIORS INVOLVING THE ARMS

Gravity-Related Arm Movements

The degree to which we move our arms is a significant and accurate indicator of our attitudes and sentiments. These movements can range from subdued (restrained and constricted) to exuberant (unrestrained and expansive). When we are happy and content, our arms move freely, even joyfully. Watch children at play. Their arms move effortlessly while they interact. You will see them pointing, gesticulating, holding, lifting, hugging, and waving.

When excited, we don't restrict our arm movements; in fact our natural tendency is to defy gravity and raise our arms high above our heads (see

---

BOX 27: **"GET YOUR HANDS IN THE AIR!"**

You don't need a gun to get people to raise their hands above their heads. Make them happy and they'll do it automatically. In fact, during a holdup is probably the *only* time individuals will simultaneously keep their hands high and be unhappy. Think of how athletes exchange high fives after a good play; watch football fans raise their arms skyward after the hometown team scores a touchdown. Gravity-defying arm actions are a common response to joy and excitement. Whether in Brazil, Belize, Belgium, or Botswana, arm waving is a truly universal display of how elated we feel.

---

box 27). When people are truly energized and happy, their arm motions defy gravity. As previously mentioned, gravity-defying behaviors are associated with positive feelings. When a person feels good or confident, he swings his arms affirmatively, such as while walking. It is the insecure person who subconsciously restrains his arms, seemingly unable to defy the weight of gravity.

Candidly tell a colleague about a drastic and costly mistake she just made at work and her shoulders and arms will sink down and droop. Ever have that "sinking feeling"? It's a limbic response to a negative event. Negative emotions bring us down physically. Not only are these limbic responses honest, but they happen in real time. We leap and thrust our arms in the air the moment the point is scored, or our shoulders and arms sink when a referee rules against us. These gravity-related behaviors communicate emotions accurately and at the precise moment we are affected. Further, these physical manifestations can be contagious, whether at a football stadium, a rock concert, or in a gathering of great friends.

Arm Withdrawal

When we are upset or fearful, we withdraw our arms. In fact, when we are injured, threatened, abused, or worried, our arms come straight to our sides or they close across our chests. This is a survival tactic that helps protect the individual when a real or perceived danger is sensed. Take, for instance, the mother who is worried about her son while he is playing with rougher children. She will often cross her arms and fold them across her abdomen. She wants to intervene but stands aside and restrains herself by holding her arms, hoping the play proceeds without injury.

When two people are arguing, they may both engage in this *arm-withdrawal behavior,* a very protective behavior of which neither party may be aware. This restraint has survival value; it protects the body while presenting a nonprovocative position. In essence, they are holding themselves back, since extending the arms might be construed as an attempt to strike and injure the other party, causing a fight to ensue.

Self-restraint can assist us not only in dealing with others but also in dealing with ourselves when we need to be comforted. For instance, injuries or pain in the torso and arms often cause us to restrict arm movement in an attempt to self-soothe or pacify. We may withdraw the arms toward the painful body region. If you have ever experienced severe intestinal distress, your arms were most likely drawn to your abdomen for comfort. At moments like this, the arms don't move outward; the limbic system requires that they attend to our needs closer to home.

Restriction of Arm Movement

Restriction of arm movements, *arm freeze*, particularly when it occurs in children, can sometimes have more sinister implications. In studying indicators of child abuse, it has been my experience that these children will restrict their arm movements in the presence of abusive parents or other predators. This makes perfect survival sense, since all animals, especially predators, orient toward movement. Instinctively, the abused child learns that the more he moves, the more likely he is to be noticed, and then potentially targeted by an abuser. So the child's limbic system instinctively self-regulates to make sure his arms do not attract attention. Arm-freeze behavior can serve to warn caring adults, whether teachers, neighbors, relatives, or friends, that a child might be the victim of abuse (see box 28).

BOX 28: **GUARDIANS ALL**

For exercise, I swim regularly at a local pool. Years ago, I became aware of a young girl who, while normally gregarious and outgoing, would restrain her arms whenever her mother was around. I noticed this response on several different days. In addition, I noted that the mother frequently spoke to this young girl using stern, caustic, and demeaning words. In the physical interactions I witnessed, she often handled her daughter roughly rather than lovingly, which was very unsettling, but not to the degree of being criminal. On the final day that I saw the girl, I noticed some bruises just above her elbows on the ventral side of her arms (the part of the arm that faces the torso when the arm is hanging normally at the side). At this point, I could no longer keep my suspicions to myself.

I notified members of the pool staff that I suspected child abuse and asked them to please keep an eye on the little girl. An employee told me she was a "special needs" child, and the bruises might be caused by her lack of coordination. I sensed that the gravity of my uneasiness wasn't registering, so I went to the director of the facility and expressed my concerns. I explained that defense wounds from falling do not manifest on the ventral side of the upper arms, but rather on the elbows or dorsal side (the outside) of the arms. Also, I knew it was not coincidence that this child looked like an automaton every time her mother came near. I was relieved to learn that this matter was later referred to authorities, after others at the swim facility made the same observations.

Let me make a very important point. If you are a parent, teacher, camp counselor, or school resource officer and you see children severely change or restrain their arm behavior around their parents or other adults, at a minimum it should arouse your interest and promote further observation. Cessation of arm movement is part of the limbic system's freeze response. To the abused child, this adaptive behavior can mean survival.

Maybe I just can't get the FBI out of me, but when I see children at a playground, I can't help but glance at their arms to note any bruises or injuries. Sadly, there is so much child abuse in the world, and during my training I was instructed to look for the signs of neglect and abuse in children and others. Not only as a result of my career in law enforcement, but also from my years as a father, I know what falling or bumping bruises look like and where they occur on the body. Bruises received through abuse are not the same. Their locations and appearance are different, and these differences can be detected by the trained eye.

As previously stated, humans use their arms to defend themselves, a predictable limbic reaction. Because children use their arms to block their bodies as their primary means of defense (adults may use objects), a flailing arm is often the first thing an abusive parent will grab. Parents who aggressively seize children in this way will leave pressure marks on the ventral side (the inside) of the arms. Especially if the parent shakes the child in this position, the marks will be deeper in color (from greater pressure) and have the larger shape of the adult hand or the elongated shape of the thumb or fingers.

While physicians and public safety officers routinely see marks such as this on young victims or patients, many of us are just not aware of their prevalence or significance. If we all learn to observe children carefully and look for the obvious signs of maltreatment, we can all help to protect innocent children. In saying this, I am not trying to make you paranoid or unreasonably suspicious, just aware. The more knowledgeable all caring adults are about the appearance of defense wounds and other abusive injuries in children, and the more we observe for such injuries, the safer our children will be. We want them to be happy and swing their arms with joy, not restrain them in fear.

Restricted arm behavior is not limited to children. It can also be seen in adults for a variety of reasons (see, for example, box 29).

A friend of mine, who was a customs inspector in Yuma, Arizona, told me that one of the things he noticed at the border was how people carried their handbags and purses when they came into the country. A person who was worried about the contents of her handbag—whether

---

BOX 29: SHOPLIFTERS' TELL

One of my earliest experiences with restrained arm behavior occurred more than thirty-five years ago at a bookstore where I was employed to spot shoplifters. From a lofty perch above the sales floor, I soon learned that these lawbreakers were relatively easy to spot. Once I understood the typical body language of shoplifters, I could identify them daily— surprisingly, even as they walked in the door. First, these individuals tended to look around a lot. Second, they tended to use fewer arm move- ments than regular shoppers. It was as though they were trying to make themselves smaller targets as they moved about the store. However, their lack of arm movements actually made them stand out more prominently— and essentially allowed me to better focus on them as they went about their larcenous ways.

---

because of their value or their illegality—tended to hold on to the bag tighter, especially as she neared the customs desk. Not only do important items tend to be better protected with the arms, but also those things we do not want noticed.

USING ARM CUES TO ASSESS FOR MOOD OR FEELINGS

If you establish an adequate baseline by observing a specific individual's arm behaviors over a period of time, you can detect how he is feeling by his arm movements. For instance, arm movements can let you know how someone is feeling upon returning home from work. After a tough day or when feeling dejected or sad, the arms will be low at the person's side, shoulders drooping. Armed with this understanding, you can comfort the person and help him or her recover from a hard day. In contrast, watch people being reunited after a long absence. They hold their open arms straight out. The meaning is clear, "Come here, I want to hold you!" This beautiful sight is reminiscent of when our own parents warmly reached out to us and we responded in kind. Our arms reach out, defying gravity and opening up our entire body, because our feelings are so genuinely positive.

What happens with our arm movements when we don't really feel positive emotions? Years ago, when my daughter was young, we were attending a family get-together, and as a relative approached me, rather than holding my arms straight out, they were only outstretched from the elbows, with my upper arms close at my sides. Interestingly, my daughter likewise adjusted her arms when this relative reached out to hug her. Subconsciously, I had transmitted that this person was welcome, but that I was not extremely excited to see her. My daughter responded in kind, later telling me that she did not like this relative, either. Whether my daughter's feelings were original or whether she had picked up on my sentiments toward this relative, we had both subconsciously demonstrated, with our less-than-stretched-out arms, how we really felt.

Arm behaviors also help to communicate such everyday messages as: "hello," "so long," "come here," "I don't know," "over there," "down here," "up there," "stop," "go back," "get out of my sight," and "I can't believe what just happened!" Many of these gestures could be understood anywhere in the world and often are employed to overcome language barriers. There are also numerous obscene gestures that involve the arms, some specific to a given culture, and others that are universally understood.

Arm Cues that Isolate

Certain arm behaviors relay the message, "Don't come close to me; don't touch!" For instance, watch some university professors, doctors, or lawyers as they walk down a hallway, or for that matter, look at the Queen of England or her husband, Prince Philip. When people place their arms behind their backs, first they are saying, "I am of higher status." Second, they are transmitting, "Please don't come near me; I am not to be touched." This behavior is often misunderstood as merely a pensive or thinking pose, but unless seen in someone studying a painting at a museum, for example, it is not. Putting the arms behind the back is a clear signal that means, "Don't get close; I don't want to make contact with you" (see figure 39). Adults can convey this message to each other and to children—even pets are sensitive to segregating gestures of the arms (see box 30). Imagine how isolating it must be for a child growing up in a household where each time he yearns to be held, his mother withdraws her arms behind her back. Such nonverbal messages, unfortunately, have lasting effects on a youngster and, all too often, like other forms of neglect and abuse, are later imitated and transmitted to the next generation.

Fig. 39

Sometimes called the "regal stance," arms behind the back mean "don't draw near." You see royalty using this behavior to keep people at a distance.

BOX 30: A PET PEEVE

Animal trainers tell me that dogs can't stand it when humans withdraw their gaze and their arms. In essence, our behavior is telling the dog, "I will not touch you." If you own a dog, try this experiment. Stand in front of your pet with your outstretched arms and hands in front of you, but not touching him. Then withdraw your arms behind your back and watch what happens. I think you'll discover the dog will react negatively.

Humans dislike it when we feel unworthy of being touched. When a couple walks together and one or the other's arms are behind the back, they are restraining themselves. Obviously, closeness or intimacy is not reflected by this behavior. Note how you feel when you extend your arm to shake someone's hand and he does not respond. When we reach out for physical contact and it is not reciprocated, we feel rejected and dejected.

There is ample scientific research that suggests that touch is very important for the well-being of humans. Health, mood, mental development, and even longevity are said to be influenced by how much physical contact we have with others and how often positive touching takes place (Knapp & Hall, 2002, 290–301). We have all read about studies where merely stroking a dog lowers a person's heart rate and serves as a calming agent. Perhaps this is true because pets are typically so unconditional in their affections that we never have to worry about reciprocation.

As a species, we have learned to use touch as a barometer of how we feel. We reach toward the things we really like and hold unpleasant things at arm's length. If you hand someone a dirty diaper for disposal, notice how the immediate reaction is to grasp it with as few fingers as possible and hold the arm away from the body. No one receives training in this, yet we all do it, because the limbic brain limits contact with objects that are disagreeable, unhealthy, or dangerous to us.

This *arm-distancing* phenomenon occurs not only when we encounter objects we don't like, but also when we are around people we don't enjoy. Our arms will act as either barriers or blocking mechanisms (like a running back stiff-arming a would-be tackler) to protect and/or distance us from threats or anything we deem negative in our environment. You can learn a lot about how a person feels about someone or something by noting whether the arm either engages or distances from the individual or object in question. Watch people at the airport or on a packed sidewalk and notice how they use their arms to protect themselves or to block others from getting too close as they make their way through the crowd. Then note how people with whom *you* interact greet you in social or business situations. I think you'll start to see that the saying "keeping someone at arm's length" has real meaning and practical consequences.

TERRITORIAL DISPLAYS OF THE ARMS

In addition to using our arms to protect us or keep people away, they can also be used to mark territory. In fact, as I am writing this paragraph, I am on an Air Canada flight to Calgary, and my very large seat neighbor and I have been jockeying for armrest territory nearly the entire flight. At the moment, I seem to be losing; I have a small corner of the armrest, but he dominates the rest and therefore my whole left side. All I can do is lean toward the window. Eventually, I decided to give up trying to carve out any additional territory, so he won and I lost. But at least I salvaged an example for this book from his territorial display. Incidents like this happen to all of us every day in elevators, doorways, or classrooms. In the end, if there is no accommodation or compromise, someone ends up being the "loser" and no one likes to feel that way.

You also see territorial displays in boardrooms or meeting rooms where one person will spread his material about and use his elbows to dominate a considerable piece of the conference table at the expense of others. According to Edward Hall, territory, in essence, is power (Hall, 1969; Knapp & Hall, 2002, 158–164). Claiming territory can have very powerful and

negative consequences—both short-lived and long-term—and the resulting battles can range from small to great. Territorial disputes encompass
everything from a turf issue on a crowded subway to the war fought between Argentina and Britain over the Falkland Islands (Knapp & Hall,
2002, 157–159). Now, here I sit, months after that flight to Calgary, and as I
edit this chapter, I can still sense the discomfort I felt when my seatmate
hogged the armrest. Clearly, territorial displays are significant to us, and
our arms help assert our dominance to others with whom we overlap in
space.

Notice how confident or high-status individuals will claim more territory with their arms than less confident, lower-status persons. A dominant man, for example, may drape his arm around a chair to let everyone
know that this is his domain or, on a first date, might confidently throw
an arm over a woman's shoulder as though she were his property. Further, with regard to "table manners," be aware that higher-status individuals will usually claim as much territory as possible immediately upon
sitting down, spreading their arms or their objects (briefcase, purse, papers) on the table. If you are new to an organization, watch for those individuals who either use their personal material (notebooks, calendars)
or their arms to claim a larger piece of real estate than most. Even at the
conference table, real estate is equated with power and status; so be observant for this nonverbal behavior and use it to assess an individual's
real or perceived status. Alternatively, the person who sits at the conference table with his elbows against his waist and arms draped between his
legs sends a message of weakness and low confidence.

Arms Akimbo

One territorial behavior used to assert dominance and project an image
of authority is known as *arms akimbo*. This nonverbal behavior involves
a person extending both arms out in a V pattern with the hands placed
(thumbs backward) on the hips. Watch police officers or military personnel in uniform when they are talking to each other. They almost always
assume the arms-akimbo posture. Although this is part of their authori-

tative training, it doesn't resonate well in the private sector. Military personnel leaving the service to enter the business world would be well advised to soften up that image so they don't come across so authoritatively (see figure 40). Minimizing arms akimbo can often ameliorate that military bearing that civilians often find disconcerting (see box 31).

For women, arms, akimbo may have particular utility. I have taught women executives that it is a powerful nonverbal display that they can employ when confronting males in the boardroom. It is an effective way for anyone, especially a woman, to demonstrate that she is standing her ground, confident, and unwilling to be bullied. Too often young women enter the

Fig. 40

Arms akimbo is a powerful territorial display that can be used to establish dominance or to communicate that there are "issues."

BOX 31: **THE WRONG ARMS OF THE LAW**

People who question the power of nonverbals to affect the behaviors of others might want to consider what happens when police use the arms-akimbo display at the wrong times. There are situations when using it can not only destroy police officers' effectiveness, but also endanger their lives.

Subconsciously, arms akimbo is a powerful display of authority and dominance, as well as a claim to territory. During a domestic dispute, if a police officer performs this display, it tends to exacerbate the feelings of those in the house and may escalate the situation. This is particularly true if the officer exhibits this posture in a doorway, blocking the exit of the homeowners. Territorial displays such as arms akimbo arouse passions, since "every man's home is his castle," and no "king" wants an outsider controlling his space.

Another potentially dangerous situation relating to the use of the arms-akimbo display involves young police officers who are taken off of their regular patrol duties to work undercover. When these undercover neophytes enter an establishment for the first time, such as a bar they are attempting to infiltrate, they may stand with arms akimbo. While this is something they are accustomed to doing, they have not earned the right to engage in such an authoritarian or territorial display among those they don't know. They advertise inadvertently that they are cops or the heat. Interviews with numerous criminals have revealed that this territorial arm display is one of the things they look for in trying to make (identify) undercover officers. Except for those in authority, most civilians rarely stand with arms akimbo. I always remind training officers and supervisors to be aware of this and make sure that undercover officers are broken of this habit so they do not give away who they are and place their lives in peril.

workplace and are bullied nonverbally by males who insist on talking to them with arms akimbo in a show of territorial dominance (see figure 41). Aping this behavior—or using it first—can serve to level the playing field for women who may be reluctant to be assertive in other ways. Arms akimbo is a good way of saying that there are "issues," "things are not good," or "I am standing my ground" in a territorial display (Morris, 1985, 195).

There is a variant to the traditional arms akimbo (which is usually performed with hands on hips with thumbs facing toward the back) in which the hands are placed on the hips, but the thumbs face forward

Fig. 41

Fig. 42

Women tend to use arms akimbo less than men. Note the position of the thumbs in this photograph.

In this photo the arms are akimbo, but note that the thumbs are forward. This is a more inquisitive, less authoritarian position than in the previous photo, where the thumbs are back in the "there are issues" position.

(see figure 41 and 42). It is often seen when people are inquisitive, yet concerned. They may approach a situation with this curious arms akimbo stance (thumbs forward, hands on hips, elbows out) to assess what is going on, and then rotate their hands to "thumbs backwards" to establish a more dominant stance of concern if necessary.

Hooding Effect

Another territorial display—similar to arms akimbo—can often be seen during business meetings and other seated social encounters when a person leans back and interlaces his hands behind his head (see figure 43). I spoke to a cultural anthropologist about this behavior, and we both concluded that it is reminiscent of the way in which a cobra "hoods" to alert other animals of his dominance and power. This *hooding effect* makes us larger than life and tells others, "I am in charge here." There is also a

Fig. 43

Interlaced hands behind the head are indicative of comfort and dominance. Usually the senior person at a meeting will pose or "hood" this way.

pecking order to this and other dominance displays. For instance, while waiting for a meeting to begin, the office supervisor may assume the interlaced hands-behind-the-head-elbows-out display. However, when the boss comes into the room, this territorial hooding display will stop. Claiming territory is for those of high status or those in charge. Thus it is the boss's right to assume this behavior while everyone else will be expected to bring their hands down to the table in an appropriate show of deference.

Dominant Pose

Often, individuals will use their arms to simultaneously emphasize a point and claim territory. This happens frequently during interactions where people are in disagreement over an issue. I recall a recent incident during a layover in New York wherein a hotel guest approached the front desk with his arms close to his body and asked the clerk on duty for a favor. When the favor was rejected, the guest shifted his request to a demand, and his arms shifted as well—spreading farther and farther apart, claiming more and more territory as the conversation became increasingly heated. This *arm spread behavior* is a powerful limbic response employed to establish dominance and emphasize a person's point of view (see figure 44). As a general rule, the meek will pull in their arms; the strong, powerful, or indignant will spread them out to claim more territory (see box 32).

In business meetings, a speaker who takes (and maintains) a large territorial footprint is likely very confident about what is being discussed (see figure 45). Spread-out arms is one of those nonverbals with high accuracy because it is limbic in origin and proclaims, "I am confident." Conversely, note how quickly someone who is splayed out over several chairs will withdraw his arms when questioned about something that makes him feel uncomfortable (see box 33).

Arm Behaviors in Courtship

In courtship behavior, the man will often be the first to put his arm around his date, particularly when there is a chance that other males

Fig. 44

Fingertips planted spread apart on a surface are a
significant territorial display of confidence and authority.

Fig. 45

Arms spread out over chairs tell the world you are feeling
confident and comfortable.

BOX 32: **SPREADING ARMS SHOULD SPREAD ALARMS**

Several years ago I was involved in training American Airlines security personnel overseas. One of the employees pointed out to me that ticket agents can often identify passengers who will become problematic by how wide they position their arms when they are at the counter. From that day forward I have looked for this behavior and have witnessed it countless times during confrontations.

I was at the airport (yes, once again!) when I overheard a passenger being told of a new regulation that required him to pay a surcharge for his overweight luggage. Immediately—as if on cue—this man splayed his arms so far apart on the counter that it actually forced him to bend at the waist. During the argument that ensued, the airline employee stepped back and crossed his arms in front of his chest and informed the passenger that unless he cooperated and calmed down he wouldn't be allowed on the airplane. Incidentally, it's not every day one gets to see two remarkable arm behaviors all at once, in what became an arm wrestling match, at a distance.

---

might try to encroach on his woman. Or he will plant an arm behind his date and pivot around her so that no one can claim or violate this territory. Watching courtship rituals can be very enlightening and entertaining—particularly when you see males subconsciously staking out their territory and their date, all at once.

Another example of courtship behaviors of the arms involves how closely a couple will (or will not) place their arms next to one another when they are seated together at a table. There are large numbers of sensory receptors in our arms, so arm touching can generate sensuous pleasure. In fact, even brushing against the hairs on our bare arms or a touch through clothing can stimulate nerve endings. So when we place our arms near someone else's, the limbic brain is demonstrating overtly that we are so comfortable, physical contact is permissible. The flip side of

---

BOX 33: **THE SWAT COMMANDER WHO PUT DOWN HIS ARMS**

Years ago, I was involved in planning a SWAT operation that was to take place in Lakeland, Florida. As the mission planner was describing the operation order, he seemed to have everything covered. His arms were outstretched over two chairs as he confidently went through the very detailed arrest plan. Suddenly someone asked, "What about the Lakeland paramedics, have they been contacted?" Instantly the mission planner withdrew his arms and dropped them between his knees, palms together. This was a significant change in territorial behavior. He went from dominating a large space to being as narrow as possible, all because he had not made the necessary arrangements. His confidence level suddenly vaporized. This is a striking example of how quickly our behaviors ebb and flow depending on our mood, level of confidence, or thoughts. These nonverbals occur in real time and immediately transmit data. When we are confident we spread out, when we are less confident we withdraw.

---

this behavior is that we will remove our arms from the vicinity of our companion's arms when the relationship is changing for the worse or when the individual with whom we are seated (whether a date or a stranger) is making us feel uncomfortable.

Adornments and Artifacts on the Arms

Around the globe, wealth is often demonstrated through the wearing of precious items or adornments on the arms. In many parts of the Middle East, it is still common for women to wear their wealth in the form of gold rings or bands on their arms, indicating relative worth and status. Men, too, will wear expensive watches to demonstrate their socioeconomic status or level of wealth. In the 1980s, men in Miami were fanatical about wearing Rolex watches; they were the status symbol du jour and were ubiquitous among drug traffickers and nouveau riche alike.

Other social emblems, including manifestations of one's personal or career history, can also be displayed in various ways on our arms. People who work in construction, athletes, and soldiers will sometimes reveal the scars of their profession. Uniforms may carry patches on the upper arms. Like the torso, the arms can be billboards to advertise aspects of our personality. Just look at the variety of tattoos people have emblazoned on their arms or the muscles that bodybuilders proudly display with tight fitting tank tops.

To the skilled observer, a careful scrutiny of people's arms can sometimes reveal information about their lifestyles. The smooth, well-manicured elbows of the pampered differ greatly from those who are scarred or tanned from daily outdoor work. People who have been in the military or in prison may have artifacts of their experiences on their arms, including scars and tattoos. Individuals who espouse hatred toward a certain group or subject will often script or tattoo evidence of that hatred on their arms. Those who use intravenous drugs may have track lines along the veins of their arms. Troubled individuals with a psychological disorder known as *borderline personality* may have cuts and slashes where they have done intentional injury to their arms (American Psychological Association, 2000, 706–707).

With specific regard to tattoos, this style of body adornment has increased in the last fifteen years, particularly in more "modernized" countries. However, this method of personal decoration has been used around the world for at least thirteen thousand years. As part of our "body billboard," the message tattoos convey in current culture should be discussed. Concurrent with the relatively recent increase in tattooing, I was involved in surveying potential jurors, specifically with regard to how a witness or a defendant would be perceived if he had tattoos. The surveys, conducted multiple times with multiple groups of men and women, concluded that tattoos were perceived by jurors as being low-status (low-class) adornments and/or vestiges of youthful indiscretion, which, in general, were not very well liked.

I tell students that if they have tattoos, they should hide them, especially when applying for a job—and particularly if going to work in the food industry or the medical profession. Celebrities may be able to get away with tattoos, but even they have them masked when working. The bottom line on the subject of tattoos is that surveys show most people don't like to see them. While that may change one day, for now, if you are trying to influence others in a positive way, you should conceal them.

Arms as Conduits of Affection

Children need to be lovingly touched so that they can grow up feeling safe and nurtured, but even adults can use a good hug every once in a while. I give hugs freely because they transmit caring and affection so much more effectively than mere words. I feel sorry for those who are not huggers; they are missing so much in their lives.

As powerful and effective as a hug can be in gaining favor and achieving interpersonal effectiveness with others, however, it can also be seen by some as an unwanted intrusion of their personal space. In the litigious age in which we live—where a well-meaning hug can be misconstrued as a sexual advance—one must be careful not to give out hugs where they are unwelcome. As always, careful observation and interpretation of people's behavior as you interact with them will be your best indicator as to whether a hug is appropriate or inappropriate in any given circumstance.

Nevertheless, even without giving a hug, people can use their arms to demonstrate warmth and, in so doing, increase their chances of being viewed favorably by others. When approaching a stranger for the first time, try demonstrating warmth by leaving your arms relaxed, preferably with the ventral side exposed and perhaps even with the palms of your hands clearly visible. This is a very powerful way of sending the message, "Hello, I mean no harm" to the other person's limbic system. It is a great way of putting the other person at ease and facilitating any interaction that follows.

In Latin America, an *abrazo* (a brief hug) is part of the culture among

---

BOX 34: DON'T GET BUGGED IF YOU GET HUGGED

Years ago at an espionage trial in Tampa, Florida, the defense attorney put me on the stand and, wishing to embarrass or discredit me, asked somewhat sarcastically, "Mr. Navarro, isn't it true that you used to hug my client, the defendant, every time you met with him?" I then replied, "It wasn't a hug, counselor, it was an abrazo, and there is a difference." I paused dramatically for a second and then continued, "It was also an opportunity for me to see if your client was armed, since he once robbed a bank." The startled defense attorney ended the provocative line of inquiry then and there, since he was not aware that his client had previously committed a bank robbery with a gun.

Interestingly, this abrazo story made the papers as though the people of Tampa and nearby Ybor City (settled by Latinos) had never heard of an abrazo. Since this trial, the attorney in question and I have become close friends and he is now a federal judge. After nearly twenty years, we still laugh about the "abrazo incident."

---

males. It is a way of saying, "I like you." In performing an abrazo, the chests come together and the arms engulf the back of the other person. Unfortunately, I know a lot of people who are reluctant to do this and/or feel very awkward when they do. I have seen American businessmen in Latin America who will either refuse to give an abrazo or when they do it, appear as though they're dancing with their grandmother. My advice is to do it and get it right, since little courtesies mean a lot in any culture. Learning a proper abrazo is no different than learning to shake hands correctly and feeling comfortable doing it. If you are a businessman and will be working in Latin America, you will be perceived as cold or aloof if you fail to learn this familiar greeting. There's no need for that when a simple gesture can engender so much good will and make you simpatico (see box 34).

SOME CONCLUDING REMARKS ABOUT
NONVERBALS OF THE ARMS

Our arms can transmit a lot of information in decoding the intentions and sentiments of others. From my perspective, one of the best ways to establish rapport with someone is to touch that person on the arm, somewhere between the elbow and the shoulder. Of course, it is always wise to assess the person's personal and cultural preferences before you proceed. Generally, however, the brief touch I have just described is usually a good and safe place to initiate human contact and to let others know you are getting along. In the Mediterranean, South American, and Arab worlds, touching is an important component of communication and social harmony. Don't be shocked, startled, or threatened as you travel if people touch you on the arm (assuming they do so appropriately, as I have described). It's their powerful way of saying, "We are OK." In fact, since human touch is so intimately involved in communication, when there is no touching between people, you should be concerned and wonder why.

SIX

Getting a Grip

Nonverbals of the Hands and Fingers

Among all species, our human hands are unique—not only in what they can accomplish, but also in how they communicate. Human hands can paint the Sistine Chapel, pluck a guitar, maneuver surgical instruments, chisel a David, forge steel, and write poetry. They can grasp, scratch, poke, punch, feel, sense, evaluate, hold, and mold the world around us. Our hands are extremely expressive; they can sign for the deaf, help tell a story, or reveal our innermost thoughts. No other species has appendages with such a remarkable range of capabilities.

Because our hands can execute very delicate movements, they can reflect very subtle nuances within the brain. An understanding of hand behavior is crucial to decoding nonverbal behaviors, for there is practically nothing your hands do that is not directed—either consciously or subconsciously—by your brain. Despite the acquisition of spoken language over millions of years of human evolution, our brains are still hardwired to engage our hands in accurately communicating our emotions, thoughts, and sentiments. Therefore, whether people are speaking or not, hand gestures merit our attention as a rich source of nonverbal behavior to help us understand the thoughts and feelings of others.

HOW APPEARANCE AND NONVERBALS OF THE HANDS AFFECT INTERPERSONAL PERCEPTION

Not only do others' hands communicate important information to us, but our own hand movements influence how others perceive us. Therefore, the way we use our hands—as well as what we learn from the hand behaviors of others—contribute to our overall interpersonal effectiveness. Let's start by examining how our hand actions affect what others think of us.

Effective Hand Movements Enhance Our Credibility and Persuasiveness

The human brain is programmed to sense the slightest hand and finger movement. In fact, our brains give a disproportionate amount of attention to the wrists, palms, fingers, and hands, as compared to the rest of the body (Givens, 2005, 31, 76; Ratey, 2001, 162–165). From an evolutionary standpoint, this makes sense. As our species adopted an upright posture and our human brain grew ever larger, our hands became more skilled, more expressive, and also more dangerous. We have a survival need to assess each other's hands quickly to see what they are saying or if they portend ill (as in holding a weapon). Because our brains have a natural bias to focus on the hands, successful entertainers, magicians, and great speakers have capitalized on this phenomenon to make their presentations more exciting or to distract us (see box 35).

People respond positively to effective hand movements. If you wish to enhance your effectiveness as a persuasive speaker—at home, at work, even with friends—attempt to become more expressive in your use of

BOX 35: **KEEPING SUCCESS WELL IN HAND**

Most successful speakers use very powerful hand gestures. Unfortunately, one of the best examples I can offer of an individual who developed his hand gestures to improve his communication skills is that of Adolf Hitler. A mere private in the First World War, a painter of greeting cards, and slight of stature, Hitler had no prequalifications or stage presence that would normally be associated with a gifted, credible orator. On his own, Hitler began to practice speaking in front of mirrors. Later, he filmed himself while practicing hand gestures to better hone a dramatic style of speaking. The rest is history. An evil human being was able to rise to prominence as leader of the Third Reich through his use of rhetorical skills. Some of the movies of Hitler practicing his hand gestures still exist in the archives. They attest to his development as a speaker who capitalized on using his hands to enthrall and control his audience.

hand movements. For some individuals, effective hand communication comes naturally; it is a gift that takes no real thought or education. For others, however, it takes concentrated effort and training. Whether you naturally speak with your hands or not, recognize that we communicate our ideas more effectively when we employ our hands.

Hiding Your Hands Creates a Negative Impression: Keep Them Visible

People may regard you with suspicion if they can't see your hands while you are talking. Therefore, always be sure to keep your hands visible during face-to-face communication with others. If you've ever talked to someone whose hands are underneath a table, I think you will quickly sense how uncomfortable the conversation feels (see box 36). When we interact in person with other individuals, we expect to see their hands, because the brain depends on them as an integral part of the communication process.

BOX 36: **AN UNDERHANDED EXPERIMENT**

Years ago I conducted an informal study in three of my classes. I asked students to interview each other, instructing half of the class to keep their hands under their desks during the conversation, while the other half was told to leave their hands visible. After a fifteen-minute interview, we discovered that the people with their hands under the desk were generally perceived as being uncomfortable, withdrawn (holding back), sneaky, or even deceptive by those with whom they were speaking. Those interviewers with their hands in plain view on top of the desk were perceived as being more open and friendly, and *none* was perceived as deceptive. Not a very scientific experiment, but quite instructive.

When conducting jury surveys, one thing that stands out is how much jurors dislike it when attorneys hide behind the lectern. Jurors want to see the attorney's hands so they can gauge the presentation more accurately. Jurors also don't like it when witnesses hide their hands; they perceive this negatively, commenting that the witness must be holding back, or perhaps even lying. While these behaviors have nothing to do with deception per se, the perception of the jurors is significant, reminding us that concealment of the hands should be avoided.

When the hands are out of sight or less expressive, it detracts from the perceived quality and honesty of the information being transmitted.

The Power of a Handshake

A handshake is usually the first—and possibly only—physical contact we have with another person. How we do it, including its strength and how long it is maintained, can affect how we are perceived by the person we are greeting. We can all remember someone who shook our hand and left us feeling uncomfortable about them or about the situation. Don't dismiss the power of a handshake to leave an impression. It is very significant.

Around the world, it is common to use the hands to greet others, although culture dictates variations on how hand greetings are performed, for how long, and how strong. When I first moved to Utah to attend Brigham Young University, I was introduced to what fellow BYU students called the "Mormon handshake." This is a very strong and lengthy handshake used extensively not only by the university students, but also by members of the Church of Jesus Christ of Latter-day Saints (Mormons). Over the years that I was there, I noticed how foreign students, in particular, were often taken aback by this rather overzealous handshake, because in many cultures, especially in Latin America, the handshake is mild (some preferring to give an abrazo, as previously mentioned).

Since handshaking is usually the first time that two people actually touch, it can be a defining moment in their relationship. In addition to being used to meet and greet, certain people use it to establish dominance. In the 1980s, much was written about how you could use the handshake to establish control and dominance by maneuvering the hand this way and that way, making sure yours was always on top. What a waste of energy!

I don't recommend hand jousting to create dominance, as our intentions should be to leave positive impressions when we meet others, not negative ones. If you feel the need to establish dominance, the hands are not the right way to do so. There are other more powerful tactics, including violation of space and eye-gaze behavior, that are more subtle.

I have shaken hands with people who try to establish dominance through this greeting, and I have always come away with negative feelings. They didn't succeed in making me feel inferior, just uncomfortable. There are also those who insist on touching the inside (ventral) side of your wrist with their index finger when they shake hands. If it is done to you and you feel uncomfortable, don't feel surprised, because most people react that way.

Similarly, you will typically feel uncomfortable if someone gives you what is referred to as a "politician's handshake," in which the other party covers the top of the handshake with his left hand. I suppose politicians think they are being friendlier with this two-handed gesture, not realizing that many people don't like being touched that way. I know people (mostly men) who insist on shaking hands this way and end up creating negative feelings in the people they meet. Obviously, you should avoid giving any of these discomforting handshakes unless you want to alienate someone.

As foreign as it may seem to Westerners, in many cultures men engage in hand-holding behavior. This is very common in the Muslim world as well as in Asia, especially in Vietnam and Laos. Men in the United States often are uncomfortable holding hands with each other because this is not common to our culture beyond childhood or perhaps in certain religious rituals. When I teach at the FBI Academy, I ask the young agents to stand and shake hands with each other. They don't have a problem doing so, even when asked to engage in a prolonged handshake. However, when I ask them to hold hands together side-by-side, sneers and objections quickly arise; they cringe at the thought, and only do so with much hesitation. Then I remind the new agents that we deal with people from many cultures and these individuals often show their comfort level with us by holding our hands. It is something we, as Americans, need to learn to accept, especially when dealing with human assets (informants) from other countries (see box 37).

Many cultures use touch to cement positive sentiments between men, something that is not widespread in the United States. The story of the Bulgarian gentleman not only reveals cultural differences but also illustrates the importance of physical contact for our species. In interpersonal relationships—whether between men, women, parents and children, or lovers—it is critical to have physical contact and to assess it to determine how the relationship stands. One of the signs that a relationship has soured or is compromised is a sudden decrease in the amount of touching (assuming it existed). In any relationship, when there is trust there is more tactile activity.

If you currently travel abroad, or plan to in the future, make sure you understand the cultural conventions of the country that you are visiting, particularly with regard to greetings. If someone gives you a weak handshake, don't grimace. If anyone takes your arm, don't wince. If you are in the Middle East and a person wants to hold your hand, hold it. If you are a man visiting Russia, don't be surprised when your male host kisses your cheek, rather than shakes your hand. All of these greetings are as natural a

---

BOX 37: WHEN CUSTOMS AND INTELLIGENCE GATHERING GO HAND IN HAND

When I was assigned to the Manhattan office of the FBI, I worked with an informant (asset) who had defected from Bulgaria. He was an older gentleman, and as time went on we became friends. I remember being at his home one afternoon, having tea, which he favored late in the day. We sat on the couch, and as he told me stories of his work and life behind the iron curtain, he took my left hand and just held it, for practically a half hour. As he spoke of his life under Soviet oppression, I could tell this encounter was more about therapy than it was about work. It was clear that this gentleman took great delight and derived much comfort from holding the hand of another person. This behavior was a sign of his trust in me as we spoke; it was much more than a routine FBI debriefing of a former intelligence officer. My acceptance of his hand was highly conducive to his coming forth with additional and vital information. I always wonder how much less information I would have received if I had moved my hand because I feared touching or holding another man's hand.

---

way to express genuine sentiments as an American handshake. I am honored when an Arab or Asian man offers to take my hand because I know that it's a sign of high respect and trust. Accepting these cultural differences is the first step to better understanding and embracing diversity.

Avoid Using Hand Gestures that Offend Others

In many countries throughout the world, finger pointing is viewed as one of the most offensive gestures a person can display. Studies show that people don't like it when someone points a finger at them (see figure 46). In schools as well as prison yards, finger pointing is often the precursor to many fights. When talking with their children, parents should be careful to avoid pointing at them while saying things like "I know you

Fig. 46

Perhaps one of the most offensive gestures we possess is finger pointing. It has negative connotations around the globe.

did it." The finger pointing is so distasteful that it may actually divert the child's attention from what is being said as they process the hostile message of the gesture (see box 38).

Finger pointing is just one of many offensive gestures a person can make with the hand or fingers. Obviously, some are so well known they need no further comment, such as "the bird." Snapping your fingers at someone is also considered rude; you should never attempt to get someone's attention with the same gesture you may use to call your dog. In the Michael Jackson trial in 2005, the jurors did not appreciate the mother of one of the victims snapping her fingers at the jury; this had a very negative effect. For those of you interested in further readings on hand gestures around the world, I would highly recommend *Bodytalk: The Meaning of Human Gestures,* by Desmond Morris, and *Gestures: The Do's and Taboos of Body Language Around the World,* by Roger E. Axtell. These two wonderful books will open your eyes to the diversity of gestures around the world and the eloquence of the hands in expressing human emotions.

BOX 38: **I DON'T GET YOUR POINT**

Research with focus groups has shown that a prosecuting attorney needs to be very careful when pointing at the defendant with the index finger during opening statements. Jurors don't like to see such behavior because, in their view, the prosecutor has not earned the right to point until he or she has proven the case. It is far better to gesture with an open hand (palm up) at the defendant than with a finger. Once the case is proven, the prosecutor can then point at the defendant with the index finger during closing arguments. This may seem trivial. However, dozens of surveys with mock jurors have shown they are sticklers on this point. So I simply tell attorneys not to engage in finger pointing in the courtroom. As for the rest of us, we should not point fingers when dealing with our spouses or children, nor with our colleagues at work. Pointing is just plain offensive.

Be Cautious When Using Preening Behaviors Involving the Hands

We use our fingers to preen our clothing, hair, and body when we are concerned with how we look. During courtship, humans engage in increased amounts of preening—not only with regard to our own appearance, but we also groom our mates. Intimacy permits the lover to gently remove a spot of lint from her male counterpart's sleeve even as he may gently dab a spot of food from the corner of her mouth. These behaviors are also seen between mother and child—not only in humans, but also in other mammals and in birds—and are indicative of caring and close intimacy. When observed within a relationship, the amount of grooming between the partners is a good barometer of their rapport and the level of intimacy permitted.

Preening, however, can also create negative perceptions. For example, it is rude and disrespectful for one person to preen herself in a

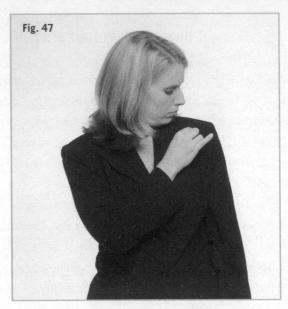

Fig. 47

Self-preening is acceptable, but not when others are talking to you. This is a sign of dismissiveness.

self-attentive, dismissive way, when she is supposed to be listening to someone else (see figure 47). In addition, there are some acts of grooming that are seen as more socially acceptable in public than others. It is fine to pick a piece of lint off your sweater on the bus, but clipping your fingernails in public is another matter. Further, what is socially acceptable preening in one setting or culture may not be seen as such in another. It is also inappropriate for a person to preen another individual when they have not reached the level of intimacy to warrant that behavior.

The Physical Appearance of Your Hands

By looking at people's hands, it is sometimes possible to assess the kind of work they do or activities in which they engage. The hands of individuals who perform manual labor will have a certain rough, calloused appearance. Scars may indicate working on a farm or athletic wounds received on the playing field. Standing with hands at the side with fingers curled may indicate prior military experience. A guitar player may have calluses on the tips of the fingers on one hand.

Hands also indicate how much we care for ourselves and how we view social convention. Hands may be tended to or they may be filthy. Nails may be manicured or look ratty. Long nails on men are seen as odd or effeminate, and people typically interpret nail-biting as a sign of nervousness or insecurity (see figure 48). Because our brains focus so much on the hands, you should pay extra attention to hand hygiene, since others will.

Learn How to Manage Sweaty Hands

No one really enjoys shaking a hand that is moist, so I advise people who develop sweaty hands when meeting others (particularly important people like potential employers, future in-laws, or individuals in a position to grant favors) to dry off their hands before they attempt a handshake. Hand sweating not only occurs when we are excessively warm, it also happens when we are nervous or under stress. When you make contact

Fig. 48

Nail-biting is generally perceived as a sign of insecurity or nervousness.

with someone who has sweaty hands, you can assume he or she is under stress (since limbic arousal causes sweating). Use this opportunity to win some interpersonal points by unobtrusively doing what you can to help the person calm down. Putting people at ease when they are stressed is one of the best ways to insure more honest, effective, and successful interactions.

There are people who erroneously believe that if you have sweaty palms, you must be lying. This is simply not accurate. The same part of the nervous system that is activated during the limbic freeze, flight, or fight response (the sympathetic nervous system) also governs our sweat glands. Since something as simple as meeting someone new can cause sweaty hands, this phenomenon *must not* be construed as indicative of deception. Approximately 5 percent of the population sweats profusely, and chronic perspiration makes the palms uncomfortably sweaty (a condition known as hyperhidrosis) (Collett, 2003, 11). Sweaty palms are not indicative of deception. They are only indicative of stress or, in some cases, a genetic disorder. Be careful when evaluating the reasons for moist hands. Although some sources state that a person is lying if his palms are sweaty, this is simply not true.

READING NONVERBALS OF THE HANDS

Up to this point, we have been examining how our hand behaviors and appearance can influence the way others perceive us. Now let's examine some nonverbals of the hands that will help us read what other people are thinking and feeling. I'll start with a few general comments about how our hands reveal information and then turn to some specific hand behaviors of high and low confidence that can be useful in understanding the people we encounter.

Nervousness in the Hands Sends an Important Message

The muscles that control our hands and fingers are designed for precise and fine movements. When the limbic brain is aroused and we are stressed and nervous, surges of neurotransmitters and hormones such as adrenalin (epinephrine) cause uncontrollable quivering of the hands. Our hands will also shake when we hear, see, or think of something that has negative consequences. Any objects held in the hands may appear to magnify this trembling, telegraphing a message that says, "I am under stress" (see box 39). This shaking behavior is particularly noticeable when a person is holding an elongated object such as a pencil or a cigarette, or something relatively large but lightweight like a piece of paper. The object will begin to shake or quiver immediately following the statement or event that created the stressful circumstances.

Positive emotions can also cause our hands to shake, whether we're holding a winning lottery ticket or a winning hand in poker. When we are genuinely excited, our hands will quiver, sometimes uncontrollably. These are limbic-driven reactions. At an airport, as parents, spouses, and other family members excitedly wait for their returning soldier or relative, their hands will often shake in excitement. They may restrain their hands by grabbing and holding someone else's hand, or by tucking their hands in their underarms or clasping them and holding them at chest level. Old videos of the Beatles' first visit to America are replete with young girls clasping their hands to combat the shaking that accompanied their extreme excitement.

Obviously, you must first determine whether shaky hands are due to fear or joy by putting the behavior in *context*—examining the circumstances in which it occurred. If the shaky hands are accompanied by pacifying actions, like touching the neck or pressing the lips together, I'd be more likely to suspect that the shaking was related to stress (something negative) rather than something positive.

It should be noted that trembling hands are only relevant as a nonverbal communication when they represent a change from someone's normal hand movements. If a person's hands always shake because, for example, he is a heavy coffee drinker or is drug or alcohol addicted, the tremor, while informative, becomes part of that individual's baseline in terms of nonverbal behavior. Likewise in people with certain neurological disorders (e.g., Parkinson's disease), hand tremor may not indicate

---

BOX 39: **WHERE THERE'S (JITTERY) SMOKE, THERE'S FIRE**

During my work on a major espionage investigation, I was interviewing a man of interest in the case. As I watched him, he lit a cigarette and began smoking. I had no real clues with regard to his possible connection to the case; there were no witnesses to the crime, no significant leads, and only vague ideas of who might be involved. During the interview I brought up many names of people who were of interest to the FBI and the army in this matter. Whenever I mentioned the name of one particular individual named Conrad, the man's cigarette shook in his hand like the needle on a polygraph machine. To see if this was a random event or something more significant, I mentioned additional names to test his reactions; there were none. Yet, on four separate occasions, when I mentioned Conrad, the subject's cigarette repeatedly shook. For me that was enough to verify there was more to the relationship between the interviewee and Conrad than we knew. The shaking of the cigarette was a limbic reaction to a threat. It was also an indication to me that this individual felt somehow endangered by the revelation of that name; therefore he likely either had knowledge of something nefarious or was directly involved in the crime.

During that initial interview with the subject, I did not know whether or not he was actually involved in the crime because, frankly, I did not know enough about the case. The only thing that spurred us to pursue the investigation and additional interviews was the fact that he had reacted to one name with the "shaky hand" response. Perhaps but for that one behavior, he would have escaped justice. In the end, after many voluntary interviews over a year, he admitted his involvement with Conrad in espionage activities and eventually gave a full confession of his crimes.

---

their emotional state. In fact, if such a person suddenly ceases to tremble for a moment, it may indicate a deliberate attempt to focus more deeply on the particular subject just mentioned (Murray, 2007). Remember, it is *change* in behavior that is most significant.

As a general guideline, any shaking behavior that starts or stops suddenly, or is somehow markedly different from baseline behavior, deserves further scrutiny. Considering the context in which the shaking occurs, when it occurs, and any other tells that might support a specific interpretation will improve your ability to read a person correctly.

HAND DISPLAYS OF HIGH CONFIDENCE

A high-confidence display reflects a high degree of brain comfort and self-assurance. Several confidence demonstrations associated with the hands alert us that the person feels good about, and comfortable with, his current state of affairs.

Steepling

Hand steepling may well be the most powerful high-confidence tell (see figure 49). It involves touching the spread fingertips of both hands, in a gesture similar to "praying hands," but the fingers are *not* interlocked and the palms may not be touching. It is called steepling because the hands look like the pointed top of a church steeple. In the United States, women tend to steeple low (perhaps at the waist), which sometimes makes the behavior more difficult to observe. Men tend to steeple higher, at chest level, which makes their steepling more visible and powerful.

Steepling signifies that you are confident of your thoughts or position. It lets others know precisely how you feel about something and how dedicated you are to your point of view (see box 40). High-status people (lawyers, judges, medical doctors) often use steepling as part of their daily behavioral repertoire because of their confidence in themselves and their status. All of us have steepled at one time or another, but we do so to varying degrees and using a variety of styles. Some do it all the time; some rarely do it; others perform modified steeples (such as with only the extended index finger and thumb touching each

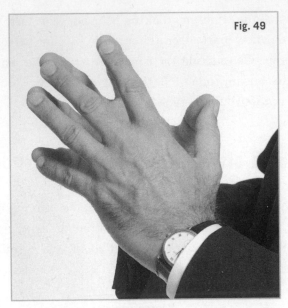

Steepling of hands, fingertip to fingertip, is one of the
most powerful displays of confidence we possess.

other while remaining fingers are interlaced). Some steeple under the
table; others do it high in front of them; some even steeple above their
heads.

In people who are unaware of the powerful nonverbal meaning of
steepling, the response can persist for significant periods of time, particularly if circumstances stay positive for them. Even when people are aware
that steepling is a tell, they still have difficulty concealing it. In these individuals, the limbic brain has made it such an automatic response that
steepling displays are difficult to overcome, because particularly when
an individual is excited, he or she forgets to monitor and control the
reaction.

Circumstances can change quickly and alter our reactions to things
and people. When this happens, we can transition from a high-confidence
steepling display to a low-confidence hand gesture in milliseconds. When
our confidence is shaken or doubt has entered our minds, our steepled
fingers may interlace as in prayer (see figure 50). These changes in

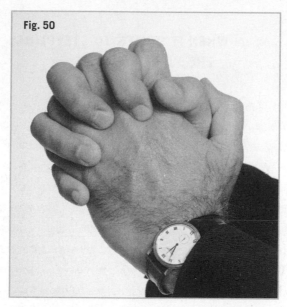

Hand-wringing is a universal way of showing we are
stressed or concerned.

nonverbal behavior happen quickly and very accurately reflect and define
our real-time internal reactions to changing events. A person can go
from steepling (high confidence) to fingers interlaced (low confidence)
and back to steepling (high confidence)—reflecting the ebb and flow of
assurance and doubt.

You, too, can harness proper steepling and hand placement for positive impact. Steepling can be such a powerful purveyor of confidence and
self-assurance that it is hard to challenge a person displaying such a nonverbal signal. Steepling is a very useful behavior to adopt; speakers and
salespeople should use it often for emphasis, as should anyone trying to
convey an important point. Consider the confidence of your hand gestures when you are being interviewed by a prospective employer, presenting material at a meeting, or simply discussing issues with your friends.

Far too often during professional meetings, I see women steepling
under the table or very low, undermining the confidence they genuinely

---

BOX 40: **WHEN IT COMES TO STEEPLING, THE JURY _ISN'T_ OUT**

The power of nonverbal behavior can be documented by studying the impact of steepling in various social settings. Steepling is useful, for example, when testifying in court; its use is advocated when training expert witnesses. Witnesses should steeple to emphasize a point or to indicate their high confidence in what they are saying. In doing so, their testimony will be perceived more powerfully by the jury than if they were merely to place their hands on their laps or interlace their fingers. Interestingly, when a prosecutor steeples as his witness testifies, the value of the testimony is enhanced because the attorney is perceived as being confident of the witness's statements. When jurors see witnesses who interlace their fingers or wring their hands, they tend to associate such behavior with nervousness or too often, unfortunately, with deception. It is important to note that both honest and dishonest individuals display these behaviors, and they should not be automatically associated with lying. It is recommended that when testifying, individuals should either steeple or cup their hands together without interlacing their fingers, as these are gestures that are perceived as being more authoritative, more confident, and more genuine.

---

possess. I hope that as they recognize the power of the steeple as an indicator of self-assurance, competence, and confidence—traits most individuals would want to be recognized as possessing—more women will embrace this gesture and display it above the table.

THUMB DISPLAYS

It is interesting how verbal language sometimes mirrors nonverbal language. When movie critics give a film two thumbs up, it indicates their

Fig. 51

Often seen with high-status individuals,
the thumb sticking out of the pocket is a
high-confidence display.

confidence in its quality. *Thumbs up* is almost always a nonverbal sign of
high confidence. Interestingly, it is also associated with high status. Look
at photographs of John F. Kennedy and notice how often he carried his
hands in his coat pocket, thumbs sticking out (see figure 51). His brother
Bobby did the same thing. Lawyers, college professors, and doctors are often seen grasping their lapels simultaneously with their thumbs up in the
air. There is a national chain of fashion/portrait studios that invariably has
females photographed with at least one hand clutching their collar with a
thumb in the air. Apparently the marketing team at this company also
recognizes that thumbs up is a high-confidence or high-status display.

High-Confidence, High-Status Thumb Displays

When individuals carry their thumbs high, it is a sign that they think highly of themselves and/or are confident in their thoughts or present circumstances (see figures 52 and 53). Thumbs up is another example of a gravity-defying gesture, a type of nonverbal behavior normally associated with comfort and high confidence. Normally, the interlacing of the fingers is a low-confidence gesture, except when the thumbs are extended straight up. It has been noted that people who use thumb displays generally tend to be more aware of their environment, more acute in their thinking, and sharper in their observations. Observe those individuals who manifest thumbs-up behavior and notice how they fit this profile. Normally, people don't posture with their thumbs up, so when they do, you can be relatively certain that this is a significant behavior indicative of positive feelings.

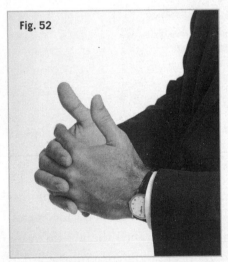

Thumbs up is usually a good indication of positive thoughts. This can be very fluid during a conversation.

The thumbs can suddenly disappear, as in this photo, when there is less emphasis or emotions turn negative.

Low-Confidence, Low-Status Thumb Displays

Feelings of low confidence can be evidenced when a person (usually a male) puts his thumbs in his pocket and lets the fingers hang out on the side (see figure 54). Particularly in an employment setting, this signal says, "I am very unsure of myself." People who are leaders or who are otherwise in control don't manifest this behavior when they are working or performing. A high-status individual who is casually relaxing may exhibit this behavior briefly, but never while he is "on." This is nearly always a low-confidence or low-status display.

Thumb displays are so accurate that they can help you effectively assess who is feeling good about himself and who is struggling. I have seen men make a potent presentation punctuated by steepling, but when a listener revealed an error in the speech, the thumbs went into

Fig. 54

Thumbs in the pocket indicate low status and confidence. People in authority should avoid this display because it sends the wrong message.

their pockets. These types of thumb displays are reminiscent of a child standing in front of a disappointed mother. This behavior conveys that someone has transitioned from high confidence to low confidence very quickly (see box 41).

BOX 41: **THUMB-THING IS WRONG HERE**

While I was staying at a world-renowned hotel in Bogotá, Colombia, the general manager commented to me that he had recently hired some new hotel guards, and although he couldn't put his finger on it, there was something about them he didn't like. He knew that I had worked in law enforcement for the FBI, and he asked whether I noticed anything bothersome about his new staff members. We walked outside where the guards were posted and took a quick glance. The manager noted that although they had new uniforms and their boots were shined, something wasn't right. I agreed that the uniforms looked professional, but pointed out that the guards were standing with their thumbs in their pockets, making them look weak and incompetent. At first the manager didn't seem to grasp what I was saying until I had him demonstrate the posture himself. Immediately he said, "You are right. They look like little kids waiting for their mother to tell them what to do." The next day the guards were shown how to stand and look authoritative (hands behind back, chin up) without looking menacing to the guests. Sometimes little things mean a lot. In this case, the disappearing thumbs became powerful purveyors of low confidence—not exactly what you want from a security force, especially in Bogotá, Colombia.

Try this experiment on your own. Stand with your thumbs in your pockets and ask people what they think of you. Their comments will confirm the unflattering and weak attitude this posture projects. You will never see a presidential candidate or a leader of a country with his thumbs in his pockets. This behavior is not seen in confident individuals (see figure 55).

Fig. 55

Often used as a sign of insecurity or social discomfort, thumbs in the pocket transmit this message readily and thus should be avoided.

Genital Framing

Men sometimes, subconsciously, will hook their thumbs inside their waistbands on either side of the zipper and either pull up their pants or even let their thumbs hang there, as their dangling fingers frame their genitals (see figure 56). *Genital framing* is a powerful dominance display. In essence, it is saying, "Check me out, I am a virile male."

Not long after starting to write this book, I discussed this nonverbal behavior when teaching a class at the FBI in Quantico, Virginia. The students scoffed, saying that no man, especially subconsciously,

Fig. 56

Using the hands to frame the genitals is often
seen with young males and females during the
courtship years. It is a dominance display.

would be that blatant about his sexuality. The very next day, one of
the students came back and told the class that he had observed a student in the bathroom who stood in front of the mirror, preened himself, put on his sunglasses, and just for a moment did some genital
framing before he proudly exited the bathroom. I am sure that the
guy wasn't even thinking about what he was doing. But in fact, genital framing occurs more often than we think, and not only in country western videos! Remember the Fonz in the TV series *Happy
Days*?

HAND DISPLAYS OF LOW CONFIDENCE OR STRESS

Low-confidence displays are the flip side of their high-confidence coun-
terparts. They reflect brain discomfort, insecurity, and self-doubt.
Low-confidence displays should alert us that the individual is experiencing negative emotions that may be caused by being in an uncomfortable situation or by thoughts that induce self-doubt or limited
confidence.

Frozen Hands

Research tells us liars tend to gesture less, touch less, and move their
arms and legs less than honest people (Vrij, 2003, 65). This is consistent
with limbic reactions. In the face of a threat (in this case having a lie detected), we move less or freeze so as not to attract attention. This behavior
is often quite observable during conversation because a person's arms
become very restrained while telling a lie and otherwise are animated
when telling the truth. Because such changes are controlled by the limbic
system rather than the thinking brain, they are more reliable and useful
than spoken words; they indicate what is really going on in the mind of
the individual who is speaking (see box 42). So look for hand and arm
movements that are suddenly restrained; they say a lot about what is going on in that person's brain.

Hand-wringing

When people wring their hands or interlace their fingers, particularly in
response to a significant comment, event, or change in their environment, it is normally indicative of stress or low confidence (see figure 50
on page 149). This common pacifier, seen in people around the world,
actually makes it look like they are engaged in prayer—and perhaps,
subconsciously or otherwise, they are. As the intensity of the hand-
wringing increases, the color of the fingers may change as areas blanch

---

BOX 42: A LESS THAN MOVING EXPERIENCE

The tendency for liars to be less animated in their gestures was a major reason I didn't believe a young woman who had told local sheriff's deputies that her six-month-old son had been kidnapped in the parking lot of a Wal-Mart in Tampa, Florida. As the woman told her story, I observed her from a monitoring room. After witnessing her behavior, I told the investigators that I didn't believe the totality of her story; her demeanor was too subdued. When people tell the truth, they make every effort to ensure that you understand them. They gesticulate with their arms and face and are emphatically expressive. Not so with this suspect. The retelling of a horrific kidnapping story by a loving and distraught mother would have been accompanied by more demonstrative, ardent behaviors. Their absence was alerting to us. Eventually the woman confessed that she had actually killed her child by stuffing him in a plastic garbage bag. The kidnapping story was a total fabrication. The freeze response of her limbic system that restrained her movements betrayed the lie.

---

due to blood being forced away from the tension points. Matters clearly are getting worse as this behavior manifests.

Interlaced Stroking or Rubbing of the Hands

A person who is in doubt (a lesser degree of lowered confidence) or under low stress will only slightly rub the palms of his hands together (see figure 57). However, if the situation becomes more stressful or if his confidence level continues to fall, watch how suddenly gentle finger-to-palm stroking transitions to more dramatic rubbing of interlaced fingers (see figure 58). The interlacing of fingers is a very accurate indicator of high distress that I have seen in the most acute of interviews—both in the FBI and in people testifying before Congress. As soon as an extremely delicate subject comes up, the fingers straighten and intertwine, as the hands

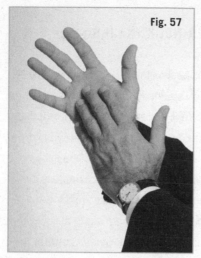

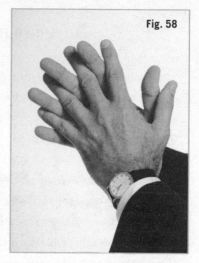

We often pacify anxiety or nervousness by stroking our fingers across the palm or rubbing our hands together.

When the fingers interlace to rub up and down, as in this photo, the brain is asking for extra hand contact to pacify more serious concerns or anxiety.

begin to rub up and down. I speculate that the increased tactile contact between the hands provides the brain with more pacifying messages.

Neck Touching

I am discussing neck touching in this chapter on hand behaviors because if you keep an eye on the hands, they eventually take you to the neck. People who touch their necks (anywhere) while speaking are, in fact, reflecting lower-than-normal confidence or are relieving stress. The covering of the neck area, throat, and/or the suprasternal notch during times of stress is a universal and strong indicator that the brain is actively processing something that is threatening, objectionable, unsettling, questionable, or emotional. It has nothing to do with deception, although deceptive people may demonstrate such behavior if they are troubled. So again, keep your eyes on the hands, and as feelings of discomfort and distress surface in people, their hands will rise to the occasion, and cover or touch their neck.

BOX 43: **UP TO HER NECK IN LIES**

Sometimes *not* covering the neck can be a telltale clue that something is amiss. I once assisted a local law enforcement agency with a case involving an alleged rape. The woman who reported this assault had reported three separate rapes in a five-year period, a statistically unlikely history. As I watched her videotaped interview, I noticed that while she spoke of how frightened she was and how terrible she felt, she was extremely passive and never once covered her suprasternal notch as she told the story. I found her "lack of behavior" suspicious and pointed it out to the investigators. The woman simply was not showing typical signs of distress. In fact, I have investigated other rape cases in which women will cover their suprasternal notch while recounting the crime even decades after it occurred. Upon further investigation, the impassive woman's case fell apart. In the end, we learned she had fabricated all her allegations—costing the city thousands of dollars—merely because she thrived on the attention given to her by responding officers, investigating detectives, and victim advocates, all of whom initially believed her and wanted to help.

I can't tell you how many thousands of times I have seen this behavior, yet most people are unaware of its significance (see box 43). Just recently I was chatting with a friend outside a conference room when a female associate walked out with one hand over her neck dimple and the other holding a cell phone. My friend continued to converse as if nothing were wrong. When the woman on the cell phone ended her call, I said, "We'd better go check on her, something's not right." Sure enough, one of her kids had come down with a high fever at school and needed to go home as soon as possible. Neck touching is one of those behaviors that is so reliable and accurate that it truly merits our close attention.

Microexpressions of the Hands

A *microgesture* is a very brief nonverbal behavior that occurs when a person is attempting to suppress a normal response to a negative stimulus (Ekman, 2003, 15). In these circumstances, the more reflexive and short-lived the behavior is, the more truthful it tends to be. For instance, let's imagine the boss tells an employee he has to help out and work this weekend because someone is sick. On hearing the news, the employee's nose crinkles or a slight smirk appears suddenly but briefly. These microgestures of dislike are very accurate displays of how the person truly feels. Similarly, our hands can display microexpressions that may surprise you (see box 44).

CHANGES IN HAND BEHAVIORS CAN REVEAL IMPORTANT INFORMATION

As with all nonverbal behaviors, sudden alterations in hand motion suggest an abrupt change in someone's thoughts and feelings. When lovers rapidly move their hands away from each other during a meal, it is a sign that something negative has just happened. Hand withdrawal may happen in seconds, but it is a very accurate real-time indicator of the person's feelings.

Gradual hand withdrawals are also worthy of note. A while ago I was invited to dinner by a married couple with whom I had been friends since our college days. We were chatting around the table at the end of the meal when the topic of finances arose. My friends revealed that they were experiencing money problems. As the wife complained about how "the money seemed to just disappear," likewise, her husband's hands simultaneously and gradually disappeared from the tabletop. As she spoke, I watched him slowly withdraw his hands until they rested, finally, on his lap. This sort of distancing is a cue indicative of *psychological flight* (part of our limbic survival mechanism) that often occurs when we are

BOX 44: **THE BIRD AS A WORD**

In his remarkable book *Telling Lies*, Dr. Paul Ekman describes his research using high-speed cameras to reveal microgestures that subconsciously communicate an individual's disfavor or true emotions (Ekman, 1991, 129–131). One such microgesture noted by Dr. Ekman is giving the bird. In a major national security case in which I was personally involved as an observer, a subject repeatedly used his middle ("bird") finger to push his glasses into position whenever the lead Justice Department interviewer (whom he despised) asked him questions. This behavior was not observed with other interviewers, but only with the interviewer the subject plainly did not like. At first we did not believe we were seeing such an obvious but fleeting gesture that was so clearly limited to a single interviewer. Fortunately, the interviews were videotaped as part of a legal proffer (i.e., the subject agrees to cooperate in consideration for a lighter sentence), so we could review the tape to confirm what we were seeing.

Perhaps equally interesting, the chief interviewer never saw the "bird" behavior and, when told about it, refused to accept that it was indicative of the interviewee's antipathy. When it was all over, however, the interviewee commented harshly on how much he despised the chief interviewer, and it was quite evident that he tried to subvert the interview because of this clash of personalities.

Microgestures of the hands come in many forms, including pushing the hands downward along the legs and then lifting the bird finger at the moment the palms reach the knees. This has been observed in both men and women. Again, these microgestures occur very quickly and can be obscured easily by other activities. Watch for these behaviors and do not dismiss them, if observed. At a minimum, microgestures should be examined in context as indicators of enmity, dislike, contempt, or disdain.

threatened. The behavior suggested to me that the husband was concealing something. As it turned out, he had been pilfering money from the
couple's joint checking account to support a gambling habit, a vice that
eventually cost him his marriage. His guilty knowledge of the covert
withdrawals explained the reason his hands withdrew from the table.
Although the motion was a gradual change, it was sufficient to cause me
to suspect that something was wrong.

One of the most important observations you can make in relation to
the hands is noticing when they go dormant. When the hands stop il-
lustrating and emphasizing, it is usually a clue to a change in brain activity (perhaps because of a lack of commitment) and is cause for heightened
awareness and assessment. Although, as we've noted, hand restriction
can signal deception, do not immediately jump to this conclusion. The
only inference you can draw at the moment the hands go dormant is that
the brain is communicating a different sentiment or thought. The change
may simply reflect less confidence or less attachment to what is being said
for a variety of reasons. Remember, any deviation from normal hand
behavior—be it an increase, a decrease, or just something unusual—
should be considered for its significance.

SOME CONCLUDING REMARKS ABOUT NONVERBALS OF THE HANDS AND FINGERS

Most of us spend so much time studying people's faces that we under-
utilize the information provided by their hands. The sensitive hands of
humans not only feel and sense the world around us, they also reflect our
responses to that world. We sit in front of a banker wondering if our
loan will be approved, with our hands in front of us, fingers intertwined
(prayerlike), reflecting the tension and nervousness within us. Or, in a
business meeting, the hands may assume a steepling position, letting others know we are confident. Our hands may quiver at the mention of
someone who betrayed us in our past. Hands and fingers can provide a

great deal of significant information. We just need to observe and decode their actions correctly and in context.

You can know how someone feels about you from a single touch. The hands are powerful transmitters of our emotional state. Use them in your own nonverbal communications and count on them to provide valuable nonverbal intelligence about others.

SEVEN

The Mind's Canvas

Nonverbals of the Face

When it comes to emotions, our faces are the mind's canvas. What we feel is exquisitely communicated through a smile, a frown, or immeasurable nuances in between. This is an evolutionary blessing that sets us apart from all other species and makes us the most expressive animals on this planet.

Our facial expressions, more than anything else, serve as our universal language—our human crosscultural lingua franca—whether here (wherever "here" is for you) or in Borneo. This international language has served as a practical means of communication since the dawn of man, to facilitate understanding among people lacking a common language.

When observing others, we can quickly recognize when someone appears surprised, interested, bored, fatigued, anxious, or frustrated. We can look at our friends' faces and see when they are displeased, doubtful, contented, anguished, disappointed, incredulous, or concerned. The expressions of children let us know if they are sad, excited, perplexed, or nervous. We were never specifically taught how to generate or translate these facial behaviors, and yet we all know them, perform them, interpret them, and communicate through them.

With all the various muscles that precisely control the mouth, lips, eyes, nose, forehead, and jaw, human faces are richly endowed to produce an immense variety of expressions. It is estimated that humans are capable of more than ten thousand different facial expressions (Ekman, 2003, 14–15).

This versatility makes nonverbals of the face very effective, extremely efficient, and, when not interfered with, quite honest. Happiness, sadness, anger, fear, surprise, disgust, joy, rage, shame, anguish, and interest are universally recognized facial expressions (Ekman, 2003, 1–37). Discomfort— whether on the face of a baby, a child, a teenager, an adult, or the elderly—is recognized around the globe; likewise we can distinguish the expressions that let us know all is well.

While our faces can be very honest in displaying how we feel, they do not always necessarily represent our true sentiments. This is because we can, to a degree, control our facial expressions and, thus, put on a false front. From an early age, we are taught by our parents not to make faces when we don't like the food in front of us, or we are compelled to fake a smile when greeting someone we don't like. In essence, we are taught to lie with our faces, and so we become quite adept at hiding our true sentiments facially, even though they occasionally do leak out.

When we lie using our faces, we are often said to be acting; obviously, world-class actors can adopt any number of faces to create fictional feelings on demand. Unfortunately, many people, especially con men and other more serious social predators, can do the same thing. They can put on a false face when they are lying, conniving, or trying to influence the perception of others through false smiles, fake tears, or deceiving looks.

Facial expressions can still provide meaningful insights into what a person is thinking and feeling. We simply have to be mindful that these signals can be faked, so the best evidence of true sentiment is derived from clusters of behaviors, including facial and body cues, that buttress or complement each other. By assessing facial behaviors in context and comparing them to other nonverbal behaviors, we can use them to help reveal what the brain is processing, feeling, and/or intending. Since the brain tends to use everything above the shoulders as a single canvas for expression and communication, we are going to refer to the face and its mantle, the neck, as one: our public face.

NEGATIVE AND POSITIVE EMOTIONAL DISPLAYS OF THE FACE

Negative emotions—displeasure, disgust, antipathy, fear, and anger—make us tense. That tension manifests in many ways in and on the body. Our faces may show a constellation of tension-revealing cues simultaneously: tightening of jaw muscles, flaring of nose wings (naral wing dilation), squinting of the eyes, quivering of the mouth, or lip occlusion (in which lips seemingly disappear). On closer examination, you might note that eye focus is fixed, the neck is stiff, and head tilt is nonexistent. An individual might not *say* anything about being tense, but if these manifestations are present there is no doubt that he is upset and that his brain is processing some negative emotional issue. These negative emotional cues are displayed similarly throughout the world, and there is real value in looking for them.

When someone is upset, either all or only a few of these nonverbal behaviors may be present, and they may manifest as mild and fleeting or may be acute and pronounced, lasting for minutes or even longer. Think of Clint Eastwood in the old spaghetti westerns, squinting at his opponents before a gun battle. That look said it all. Of course actors are trained to make their facial expressions particularly easy to recognize. However, in the real world, these nonverbal cues are sometimes more difficult to spot, either because they are subtle, intentionally obfuscated, or simply overlooked (see figure 59).

Consider, for example, *jaw tightening* as an indication of tension. After a business meeting, an executive might say to a colleague, "Did you

Squinting, furrowing of the forehead, and
facial contortions are indicative of distress
or discomfort.

see how tense Bill's jaw got when I made that proposal?" Only to hear
his partner respond, "No, I didn't catch that" (see box 45). We miss facial
cues because we have been taught not to stare and/or because we concentrate more on *what* is being said than on *how* it is being said.

Keep in mind that people often work at hiding their emotions, making them more difficult to detect if we are not conscientious observers. In
addition, facial cues may be so fleeting—microgestures—that they are
difficult to pick up. In a casual conversation, these subtle behaviors may
not be of much significance, but in an important interpersonal interaction (between lovers, parents and children, business associates, or at an
employment interview), such seemingly minor displays of tension may
reflect deep emotional conflict. Since our conscious brains may try to
mask our limbic emotions, any signals that reach the surface are critical to detect, as they may yield a more accurate picture of a person's
deep-rooted thoughts and intentions.

Although many joyous facial expressions are easily and universally
recognized, these nonverbal tells may also be suppressed or concealed for

---

**BOX 45: MY LIPS SAY I LOVE YOU, BUT MY LOOKS
SAY OTHERWISE**

I am amazed at how many times positive words pour from people's mouths while their faces gives off negative nonverbals that clearly contradict what is being said. At a recent party, one of the guests was commenting how pleased he was that his kids had good jobs. He said this, with a less-than-generous smile and tight jaw muscles, as those standing around congratulated him. Later, his wife told me privately that her husband was, in fact, extremely upset that the kids were just barely getting by in their meaningless jobs that were going nowhere. His words said one thing, but his face said quite another.

---

a variety of reasons, making them more difficult to detect. For example, we certainly don't want to show elation when we are dealt a powerful hand of cards in a poker game, or we may not want our colleagues to know we received a larger financial bonus than they did. We learn to try to conceal our happiness and excitement in circumstances where we deem it unwise to reveal our good fortune. Nevertheless, as with negative body cues, subtle or restrained positive nonverbals can be detected through careful observation and assessment of other subtle corroborative behaviors. For instance, our faces may leak a twinge of excitement that by itself, might not be enough to convince an astute observer that we are truly happy. However, our feet might provide additional corroborative evidence of excitement, helping to validate the belief that the positive emotion is genuine (see box 46).

Genuine and unrestrained feelings of happiness are reflected in the face and neck. Positive emotions are revealed by the loosening of the furrowed lines on the forehead, relaxation of muscles around the mouth, emergence of full lips (they are not compressed or tight lipped), and widening of the eye area as surrounding muscles relax. When we are truly

---

BOX 46: **THE FACE AND FEET SHOW LIFE IS SWEET**

Not long ago I was waiting for a flight out of Baltimore when the man next to me at the ticket counter received the good news that he was being upgraded to first class. As he sat down he tried to suppress a smile, since to gloat over his good fortune would be seen as rude by other passengers waiting for an upgrade. Based on his facial expression alone, to declare he was happy would have been a marginal call. Then, however, I overheard him call his wife to tell her the good news, and although he spoke quietly so those seated nearby couldn't hear the conversation, his feet were bouncing up and down like those of a young child waiting to open his birthday gifts. His happy feet provided collaborative evidence of his joyful state. Remember, look for clusters of behavior to solidify your observations.

---

relaxed and comfortable, facial muscles relax and the head will tilt to the side, exposing our most vulnerable area, the neck (see figure 60). This is a high-comfort display—often seen during courtship—that is nearly impossible to mimic when we are uncomfortable, tense, suspicious, or threatened (see box 47).

INTERPRETING NONVERBAL BEHAVIORS OF THE EYES

Our eyes have been called the windows of the soul, so it seems appropriate to examine these two portals for nonverbal messages of emotions or thoughts. Despite music lyrics such as "your lyin' eyes," our eyes do express a lot of useful information. In fact, the eyes can be very accurate barometers of our feelings because, to some degree, we have very little control over them. Unlike other areas of the face that are far less reflexive in their movements, evolution has modified muscles in and around the

---

BOX 47: WHAT YOU WON'T SEE IN AN ELEVATOR

Try to tilt your head in an elevator full of strangers and leave it that way for the complete duration of the ride. For most people this is extremely diffi-cult to accomplish, because head tilt is a behavior reserved for times when we are truly comfortable—and standing in an elevator surrounded by strangers is certainly *not* one of those times. Try tilting your head while looking directly at someone in the elevator. You will find that even more difficult, if not impossible.

---

eyes to protect them from hazards. For example, muscles inside the eye-ball protect the delicate receptors from excessive light by constricting the pupil, and muscles around the eyes will close them immediately if a dan-gerous object comes near. These automatic responses help make the eyes a very honest part of our face, so let's examine some specific eye behaviors

Fig. 60

Head tilt says in a powerful way, "I am comfortable, I am receptive, I am friendly." It is very difficult to do this around people we don't like.

that can help us achieve insight into what people are thinking and how they intend to act.

Pupilary Constriction and Squinting as a Form of Eye Blocking

Research has shown that once we move beyond a startle response, when we like something we see, our pupils dilate; when we don't, they constrict (see figure 61) (Hess, 1975a; Hess, 1975b). We have no conscious control over our pupils, and they respond to both external stimuli (for example, changes in light) and internal stimuli (such as thoughts) in fractions of a second. Because the pupils are small and difficult to see, particularly in dark eyes, and since changes in their size occur rapidly, pupil reactions are difficult to observe. Although these eye behaviors are very useful, people often don't look for them, ignore them, or, when they see them, undervalue their utility in assessing a person's likes and dislikes.

When we become aroused, are surprised, or are suddenly confronted, our eyes open up—not only do they widen, but the pupils also quickly dilate to let in the maximum amount of available light, thus sending the maximum amount of visual information to the brain. Obviously, this startle response has served us well over millennia. However, once we have a moment to process the information and if it is perceived negatively (it is an unpleasant surprise or an actual threat), in a fraction of a second the pupils will constrict (Ekman, 2003, 151) (see box 48). By constricting the

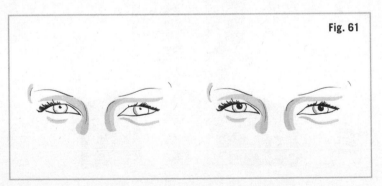

Fig. 61

In this diagram you can see pupil dilation and constriction. From birth we find comfort in dilated pupils, especially those with whom we are emotionally attached.

BOX 48: IF THEY CONSTRICT, YOU CAN CONVICT

In 1989, while working with the FBI on a matter involving national security, we repeatedly interviewed a spy who, while being cooperative, was nevertheless reluctant to name his co-conspirators involved in espionage. Attempts to appeal to his sense of patriotism and his concern for the millions of people he was placing in harm's way got us nowhere; things were at an impasse. It was essential that this man's other associates be identified; they were still at large and presented a serious threat to the United States. Left with no alternatives, Marc Reeser, a friend and brilliant intelligence analyst with the FBI, suggested using nonverbals in an attempt to glean the information we needed.

We presented this spy with thirty-two three-by-five-inch cards prepared by Mr. Reeser, each with the name of someone with whom the felon had worked, and who potentially could have assisted him. As he looked at each card, the man was asked to tell, in general terms, what he knew about each individual. We weren't specifically interested in the man's answers, since clearly words can be dishonest; rather, we were watching his face. When he saw two names in particular, his eyes first widened in recognition, and then his pupils quickly constricted and he squinted slightly. Subconsciously, he clearly did not like seeing these two names and somehow felt in danger. Perhaps those individuals had threatened him not to reveal their names. This pupilary constriction and slight squinting were the only clues we had as to the identity of his co-conspirators. He was not aware of his nonverbal signals, and we did not comment on them. However, had we not looked for this eye behavior, we never would have identified those two individuals. The two accomplices were eventually located and interviewed, at which time they confessed their involvement in the crime. To this day, the subject of that interview does not know how we were able to identify his fellow culprits.

pupils, everything in front of us thus becomes precisely focused so that we can see clearly and accurately in order to defend ourselves or effectively escape (Nolte, 1999, 431–432). This is very similar to how a camera aperture (opening) works: the smaller the aperture, the greater the depth of field, and the clearer the focus on everything near and far. Incidentally, if you ever need an emergency pair of reading glasses and none are available, just make a small pinhole in a piece of paper and hold it up to your eye; the small aperture will bring what you are reading into focus. If maximal pupil constriction isn't sufficient, then we squint to make the aperture as small as possible while simultaneously protecting the eye (see figure 62).

While walking with my daughter a few years back, we passed someone she recognized. She squinted slightly as she gave the girl a low wave. I suspected something negative had transpired between them, so I asked my daughter how she knew the girl. She replied that the girl had been a high school classmate with whom she had previously had words. The low-hand wave was done out of social convention; however, the eye squint was an honest and betraying display of negative emotions

Fig. 62

We squint to block out light or objectionable things. We squint when we are angry or even when we hear voices, sounds, or music we don't like.

Fig. 63

Squinting can be very brief—1/8 of second—but in real time may reflect a negative thought or emotion.

and dislike (seven years in the making). My daughter was unaware that her squinting behavior had given away her true feelings about the girl, yet the information stood out like a beacon to me (see figure 63).

The same phenomenon is seen in the business world. When customers or clients suddenly squint while reading a contract, they are likely struggling with something in the wording of the text, the discomfort or doubt registering immediately in their eyes. Most likely these business associates will be totally unaware they are transmitting this very clear message of disagreement or dislike.

In addition to squinting when ill at ease, some individuals will lower their eyebrows after observing something unsettling in their environment. Arched eyebrows signify high confidence and positive feelings (a gravity-defying behavior), whereas lowered eyebrows are usually a sign of low confidence and negative feelings, a behavior that indicates weakness and insecurity in a person (see box 49).

Eye Blocking, or How the Brain Spares Itself

Our eyes, more remarkable than any camera, have evolved as the primary means by which humans receive information. In fact, we often
attempt to censor incoming data through a limbic survival mechanism
known as *eye blocking*, which evolved to protect the brain from "seeing"
undesirable images. Any decrease in the size of the eyes, whether through
squinting or pupilary constriction, is a form of subconscious blocking
behavior. And all blocking behaviors are indicative of concern, dislike,
disagreement, or the perception of a potential threat.

The many forms of eye blocking are such a common and natural part
of our nonverbal repertoire that most people either miss them completely
or ignore their meaning (see figures 64–67). For example, think about a
time when someone told you bad news. Perhaps you didn't notice, but

Fig. 64

Eye blocking with the hands is an effective way of saying, "I don't like what I just heard, saw, or learned."

Fig. 65

A brief touch of the eyes during a conversation may give you a clue to a person's negative perception of what is being discussed.

Fig. 66

A delay in opening of the eyelids upon hearing information or a lengthy closure is indicative of negative emotions or displeasure.

Fig. 67

Where the lids compress tightly as in this photo, the person is trying to block out totally some negative news or event.

most likely as you heard the information your eyelids closed for a few moments. This type of blocking behavior is very ancient in origin and hardwired in our brains; even babies innately eye block within the womb when confronted with loud sounds. Even more amazing is the fact that children who are born blind will cover their eyes when they hear bad news (Knapp & Hall, 2002, 42–52). Throughout our lives we employ this limbic-driven eye-blocking behavior when we hear something terrible, despite the fact that it neither blocks our hearing nor the thoughts that follow. Perhaps it simply serves to give the brain a temporary respite or to communicate our deepest sentiments, but regardless of the reason, the brain still compels us to perform this behavior.

Eye blocking takes many forms and can be observed at any tragic event, whether bad news is being broadcast or as tragedy is about to befall us. People may cup a hand completely over both eyes, put one open hand over each eye, or block the entire face with an object, such as a newspaper or book. Even internal information in the form of a thought can compel this response. A person who suddenly remembers he forgot something important may momentarily close his eyes and take a deep breath as he ponders his blunder.

When interpreted in context, eye-blocking behaviors can be powerful indicators of a person's thoughts and feelings. These distancing clues occur in real time as soon as something negative is heard. During conversation, this is one of the best signals to let us know that something spoken did not sit well with the person hearing the information.

I have repeatedly used eye-blocking behavior as a tell in my work with the FBI. The "ice-pick" murder and the hotel fire in Puerto Rico, discussed earlier in this book, are only two of the many, many times I witnessed the significance of this eye behavior. I still watch for eye-blocking behavior on a daily basis to assess the feelings and thoughts of others.

While eye-blocking behaviors are usually associated with seeing or hearing something negative that causes us discomfort, they can also be an indication of low confidence. As with most other tells, the eye-blocking response is most reliable and valuable when it happens immediately after a significant event that you can identify. If an eye block occurs right after you tell a person a specific piece of information, or upon making some type of an offer, it should tell you that something is amiss and the individual is troubled. At this point, you might want to rethink how you wish to proceed if your goal is to enhance your chances of interpersonal success with this person.

Pupilary Dilation, Eyebrow Arching, and Flashbulb Eyes

There are plenty of eye behaviors that show positive feelings. At a very young age, our eyes register comfort when we see our mothers. A baby will follow his mother's face within seventy-two hours of birth, and his eyes will widen when she enters the room, demonstrating interest and contentment. The loving mother will likewise exhibit a relaxed opening of her eyes, and the baby will gaze into them and take comfort from her. Widened eyes are a positive sign; they indicate that someone is observing something that makes her feel good.

Contrary to pupil constriction, contentment and positive emotions are indicated by pupil dilation. The brain is essentially saying, "I like what I see; let me see it better!" When people are truly pleased by what they see, not only do their pupils dilate, but their eyebrows rise (arch), widening their eye area and making their eyes look larger (see figures 68, 69, 70) (Knapp & Hall, 2002, 62–64). In addition, some people dramatically expand the aperture of their eyes by opening their eyes as big and wide as possible, creating an appearance known as *flashbulb eyes*. This is the wide-eyed look normally associated with surprise or positive events (see box 50). This is also another form of the gravity-defying behaviors usually associated with good feelings.

Eye Flash

A variant on the flashbulb eyes is the eyebrow raise or *eye flash* that takes place very quickly, staccato-like, during a positive emotional event. Not only is this behavior universally recognized as indicative of a pleasant surprise (think of someone arriving at a surprise party), but it is also used

Fig. 68

When we are content, our eyes are relaxed and show little tension.

Fig. 69

Here the eyebrows are arched slightly, defying gravity, a sure sign of positive feelings.

Fig. 70

Flashbulb eyes can be seen when we are excited to see someone or are full of positive emotions we just can't hold back.

BOX 50: **WHEN THE FLASHBULB GOES OFF**

When we see someone we like or are surprised by running into a person we haven't seen in a while, we tend to expand our eyes to make them as big as possible, concurrent with pupilary dilation. In a work environment, you can assume the boss really likes you or that you did something really well if his or her eyes open very wide when looking at you.

You can use this affirming behavior to determine if you are on the right track, whether courting, doing business, or just trying to make friends. For example, picture the exaggerated dreamy eyes of a young girl in love as she stares at her date with adoration. In short, watch the eyes—the bigger they get, the better things are! On the other hand, when you start to see eye shrinkage, such as squinting, eyebrows dropping, or pupils constricting, you may want to rethink and change your behavioral tactics.

I will express a note of caution. Pupil dilation and constriction can be caused by factors unrelated to emotions or events, such as variation in lighting, some medical conditions, and certain drugs. Be careful to consider these factors, or you could be misled.

---

for emphasis, and to show intensity. It is very common to see people saying, "Wow!" as they raise their eyebrows and flash their eyes. This is a very genuine positive display. When someone is excitedly emphasizing a point or telling a story, the brow raise should occur. It reflects the true mood of the individual, and it also clears the way for greater visual clarity.

Perhaps the best utility of the brow raise is to note when someone stops doing it while telling a story. Often, when we are not emotionally attached to something being said, there will be no eye emphasis. Such an observed lack of attachment may simply reflect decreased interest or may occur because what is being said is not the truth. Distinguishing between these causes is difficult; essentially all you can do is look for a decrease in brow raises, or their sudden absence, to alert you that something has changed. It is remarkable how often people will change their facial emphasis (their eyebrow flashes) as they become less and less committed to what they are saying or doing.

Eye-Gaze Behavior

It is universal that when we look directly at others, we either like them, are curious about them, or want to threaten them. Lovers stare into each other's eyes with great frequency, as do mother and child; but so do predators who use a direct gaze to either mesmerize or threaten (think of stares of Ted Bundy and Charles Manson). In other words, the brain employs a single eye behavior—a strong gaze—to communicate love, interest, or hate. Therefore, we must rely on other facial displays that accompany *eye-gaze behavior* to determine liking (a relaxed smile) or dislike (tightened jaws, compressed lips).

Conversely, when we gaze away during a conversation, we tend to do so to engage a thought more clearly without the distraction of looking at the person with whom we are talking. This behavior is often mistaken as rudeness or as personal rejection, which it is not. Nor is it a sign of deception or disinterest; in fact, it is actually a *comfort display* (Vrij, 2003, 88–89). When talking to friends, we routinely look in the distance as we converse. We do this because we feel comfortable enough to do so; the limbic brain detects no threats from this person. Do not assume someone is being deceptive, disinterested, or displeased just because he or she looks away. Clarity of thought is often enhanced by looking away, and that is the reason we do it.

There are many other reasons for looking away from a speaker. A downward gaze may demonstrate that we are processing a sentiment or a feeling, conducting an internal dialogue, or perhaps demonstrating submissiveness. In many cultures, a downward gaze or other form of *eye aversion* is expected in the face of authority or in the presence of a high-status individual. Often children are taught to look down humbly when being chastised by a parent or adult (Johnson, 2007, 277–290).

In embarrassing situations, onlookers may avert their eyes out of courtesy. Never assume that a downward gaze is a sign of deception.

In all cultures in which it has been studied, science validates that those who are dominant have more freedom in using eye-gaze behavior. In essence, these individuals are entitled to look wherever they want. Subordinates, however, are more restricted in where they can look and when. Humility dictates that in the presence of royalty, as in church, heads are bowed. As a general rule, dominants tend to ignore subordinates visually while subordinates tend to gaze at dominant individuals at a distance. In other words, higher-status individuals can be indifferent while lower-status persons are required to be attentive with their gaze. The king is free to look at anyone he wants; but all subjects face the king, even as they back out of a room.

Many employers have told me that they dislike it during an interview when applicants' eyes are wandering all over the room "as though they own the place." Because roving eyes make a person look disinterested or superior, doing so always leaves a bad impression. Even if you are attempting to ascertain whether or not you would like to work there, you will likely never get the chance if your eyes do not focus on the person speaking during a job interview.

Eye-Blink / Eye-Flutter Behavior

Our blink rate increases when we are aroused, troubled, nervous, or concerned, and it returns to normal when we are relaxed. A series of rapid eye blinks may reflect an inner struggle. For instance, if someone says something we don't like, we may actually flutter our eyelids. Similarly, we might also do so if we are having trouble expressing ourselves in a conversation (see box 51). Eyelid flutter is very much indicative of a struggle either with our performance or with the delivery or acceptance of information. Perhaps more than any other actor, British actor Hugh Grant uses eyelid flutter to communicate that he is befuddled, nonplussed, struggling, or otherwise in trouble.

Students of nonverbal communication often note how President

BOX 51: FLUTTER FOCUS

Observing for eyelid flutter can help you read people and adjust your behavior accordingly. For instance, in a social gathering or business meeting, the socially adept will look for this behavior to assess participants'
comfort. Something is troubling the individual whose lids are quivering.
This nonverbal is very accurate, and in some people it will start precisely
at the moment an issue arises. For instance, in conversation, an onset of
eyelid flutter indicates the subject has become controversial or unacceptable and a change of topic is probably in order. The sudden appearance
of this nonverbal signal is important and should not be ignored, if you
want your guests to be comfortable. Since people vary in their blink rate
or eyelid fluttering—particularly if they are adjusting to new contact
lenses—you should look for changes in flutter rate, such as a sudden
absence or increase in flutter, to gain insight into a person's thoughts and
feelings.

Richard Nixon's blink rate increased when he made his "I am not a
crook" speech. The fact is eye-blink frequency will likely increase in anyone under stress whether he is lying or not. I reviewed President Bill
Clinton's eye-blink rate during his deposition, and it increased fivefold as
a result of the stress he was under. Though it's tempting to do so, I would
be very reluctant to label anyone a liar just because their blink rate increases, since any stress, including being asked questions in public, can
cause the blink rate to increase.

Looking Askance

Looking *askance* at others is a behavior that is performed with the head
and eyes (see figure 71). It can take the form of a sideways or tilted head
motion accompanied by a side glance or a brief roll of the eyes. Looking
askance is a display that is seen when we are suspicious of others or

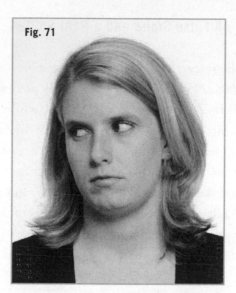

Fig. 71

We look askance at people when we are distrustful or unconvinced, as in this photo.

question the validity of what they are saying. Sometimes this body signal is very quick; at other times it may be almost sarcastically exaggerated and last throughout an encounter. While more curious or wary than clearly disrespectful, this nonverbal is fairly easy to spot and its message is, "I am listening to you but I am not buying what you're saying—at least not yet."

UNDERSTANDING NONVERBAL BEHAVIORS OF THE MOUTH

Like the eyes, the mouth provides a number of relatively reliable and noteworthy tells that can assist you in dealing more effectively with people. Like the eyes, the mouth can also be manipulated by the thinking brain to send out false signals, so caution must be exercised in interpretation. That said here are some focal points of interest with regard to the body language of the mouth.

A False Smile and a Real Smile

It is well known by researchers that humans have both a fake and a real smile (Ekman, 2003, 205–207). The fake smile is used almost as a social obligation toward those who are not close to us, while the real smile is reserved for those people and events we truly care about (see box 52).

A real smile appears primarily because of the action of two muscles: the *zygomaticus major,* which stretches from the corner of the mouth to the cheekbone, and the *orbicularis oculi*, which surrounds the eye. When working together bilaterally, these draw the corners of the mouth up and crinkle the outer edges of the eyes, causing the crow's feet of a familiar warm and honest smile (see figure 72).

BOX 52: THE SMILE BAROMETER

With practice, it won't take you long to distinguish between a fake smile and the real thing. One easy way to speed the learning process is to watch how people you know greet others based on how they feel about them. For example, if you know your business partner feels good about individual A and dislikes individual B and both have been invited to an office party he is hosting, watch his face as he meets each person at the door. You'll be able to distinguish the two types of smiles in no time at all!

Once you can distinguish between a false and real smile, you can use it as a barometer of how people *really* feel about you and you can respond accordingly. You can also look for the different types of smiles to gauge how your ideas or suggestions are coming across to the listener. Ideas that are greeted with genuine smiles should be explored further and put on the fast-track to-do list. Suggestions that are met with the fake smile should be reevaluated or put on the back burner.

This smile barometer works with friends, spouses, co-workers, children, and even your boss. It provides information about people's feelings in all types and phases of interpersonal interaction.

Fig. 72

Fig. 73

A real smile forces the corners of the mouth up toward the eyes.

This is a fake or "polite smile": the corners of the mouth move toward the ears and there is little emotion in the eyes.

When we exhibit a social or false smile, the lip corner stretches sideways through the use of a muscle called the *risorius*. When used bilaterally, these effectively pull the corners of the mouth sideways but cannot lift them upward, as is the case with a true smile (see figure 73). Interestingly, babies several weeks old will already reserve the full zygomatic smile for their mothers and utilize the risorius smile for all others. If you are unhappy, it is unlikely that you will be able to smile fully using both the zygomaticus majoris and the orbicularis oculi muscles. Real smiles are difficult to fake when we have a sincere lack of emotion.

Disappearing Lips, Lip Compression, and the Upside-Down U

If it seems like the lips have disappeared from every photograph you have seen recently of anyone testifying before Congress, it is because

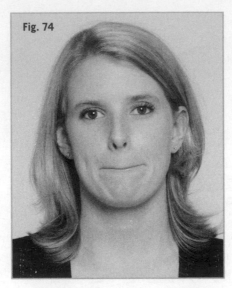

When the lips disappear, there is usually
stress or anxiety driving this behavior.

of stress. I say this with assurance, because when it comes to stress
(like testifying before Congress), nothing is more universal than
disappearing lips. When we are stressed, we tend to make our lips
disappear subconsciously.

When we press our lips together, it is as if the limbic brain is telling us
to shut down and not allow anything into our bodies (see figure 74), because at this moment we are consumed with serious issues. Lip compression is very indicative of true negative sentiment that manifests quite
vividly in real time (see box 53). It is a clear sign that a person is troubled
and that something is wrong. It rarely, if ever, has a positive connotation.
This does not mean the person is being deceptive. It just means that they
are stressed at the moment.

In the following series of photographs (see figures 75–78), I
demonstrate how the lips progressively go from full (things are OK) to
disappearing or compressed lips (things are not OK). Note especially
on the final photograph (figure 78) how the corner of the mouth turns
down, making the mouth look like an upside-down U. This behavior

---

BOX 53: **WHEN DISAPPEARING LIPS AREN'T THE ONLY THINGS BEING HIDDEN**

I look for lip compression or disappearing lips during interviews or when someone is making a declarative statement. This is such a reliable cue that it will show up precisely at the moment a difficult question is asked. If you see it, that doesn't necessarily mean the person is lying. Instead, it indicates that a very specific question served as a negative stimulus and really bothered the person. For example, if I ask someone, "Are you hiding something from me?" and he compresses his lips as I ask the question, he *is* hiding something. This is especially accurate if it is the only time he has concealed or compressed his lips during our discussion. It is a signal that I need to push further in questioning this person.

---

is indicative of *high distress* (discomfort). This is a formidable cue or signal that the person is experiencing an extreme amount of stress.

In my classes (you might want to try this with friends), I tell students to make their lips disappear or compress them and to look around at each other. What they soon realize, when I point it out to them, is they can make their lips disappear, but usually it is in a straight line. Most people who try this cannot force the corners of the mouth down into an upside-down U shape. Why? Because this is a limbic response that is hard to mimic unless we are really distressed or grieving. Do keep in mind that for some people, the turned-down corners of the mouth is a normal behavior and as such is *not* an accurate sign of distress. However, for the large majority of us, this is a very accurate tell of negative thoughts or sentiments.

The Lip Purse

Be sure to look for individuals who purse their lips while you or someone else is talking (see figure 79). This behavior usually means they disagree with

Fig. 75

Note that when the lips are full, usually the person is content.

Fig. 76

When there is stress, the lips will begin to disappear and tighten.

Fig. 77

Lip compression, reflecting stress or anxiety, may progress to the point where the lips disappear, as in this photo.

Fig. 78

When the lips disappear and the corners of the mouth turn down, emotions and confidence are at a low point, while anxiety, stress, and concerns are running high.

Fig. 79

We purse our lips or pucker them when we are in disagreement with something or someone, or we are thinking of a possible alternative.

what is being said or they are considering an alternative thought or idea. Knowing this information can be very valuable in helping you determine how to present your case, modify your offer, or guide the conversation. To ascertain whether the lip purse means disagreement or rather that the person is considering an alternative point of view, you should monitor the ongoing conversation long enough to gather additional clues.

Lip pursing is often seen during closing arguments at a trial. While one attorney speaks, the opposing counsel will purse his or her lips in disagreement. Judges also do it as they disagree with attorneys during side-bar conferences. While reviewing contracts, watching for—and spotting—lip-pursing behaviors can help attorneys decipher the concerns or issues of opposing counsel. Lip pursing can be seen during police interviews, especially when confronting a suspect with the wrong information. The suspect will purse his lips in disagreement because he knows the investigator has the facts wrong.

In business settings, lip pursing occurs all the time and should be considered an effective means of gathering information about a situation. For example, as a paragraph is being read from a contract, those opposed to a particular item or sentence will purse their lips at the very moment the words are uttered. Or, as individuals are being mentioned for promotion, you will see lip pursing as the name of someone less desirable is being mentioned.

Lip pursing is so accurate that it really should be given greater attention. It shows up in numerous settings and circumstances and is a very reliable indicator that a person is thinking alternatively or is completely rejecting what is being said.

The Sneer

The sneer, like the rolling of the eyes, is a universal act of contempt. It is disrespectful and reflects a lack of caring or empathy on the part of the person doing the sneering. When we sneer, the *buccinator muscles* (on the sides of our face) contract to draw the lip corners sideward toward the ears and produce a sneering dimple in the cheeks. This expression is very visible and meaningful even if it is flashed for just a moment (see

Fig. 80

A sneer fleetingly signifies disrespect or disdain. It says "I care little for you or your thoughts."

BOX 54: NOTHING TO SNEER AT

At the University of Washington, researcher John Gottman discovered during therapy with married couples that if one or both partners sneered, this was a significant and "potent signal" for predicting the likelihood of a breakup. Once disregard or contempt has entered the psyche, as indicated by a sneer, the relationship is troubled or even terminal. I have noted during FBI investigations that suspects will sneer during interviews when they think they know more than the interviewer or sense that the officer does not know the full picture. In either circumstance, a sneer is a distinct sign of disrespect or contempt for another person.

---

figure 80). A sneer can be very illuminating with regard to what is going on in a person's mind and what that may portend (see box 54).

Tongue Displays

There are numerous tongue signals that can provide us with valuable insights into a person's thoughts or moods. When we are stressed, causing our mouth to be dry, it is normal to lick our lips to moisten them. Also, during times of discomfort, we tend to rub our tongues back and forth across our lips to pacify and calm ourselves. We may stick out the tongue (usually to the side) as we focus assiduously on a task (for example when basketball great Michael Jordan goes up for a dunk) or we may poke out our tongue to antagonize someone we dislike or to show disgust (children do this all the time).

When an individual displays other mouth cues associated with stress, such as lip biting, mouth touching, lip licking, or object biting, it further bolsters a careful observer's belief that the person is insecure (see figure 81). Additionally, if people touch and/or lick their lips while pondering their options, particularly when they take an unusual amount of time, these are signs of insecurity.

Fig. 81

Lip licking is a pacifying behavior that
tends to soothe and calm us down. You
see it in class just before a test.

Tongue-jutting behavior is a gesture used by people who think they
have gotten away with something or are caught doing something. I have
seen this behavior in flea markets both here and in Russia, among street
vendors in Lower Manhattan, at poker tables in Las Vegas, during interviews at the FBI, and in business meetings. In each case, the person
made the gesture—tongue between the teeth without touching the
lips—at the conclusion of some sort of a deal or as a final nonverbal
statement (see figure 82). This, in its own way, is a transactional behavior. It seems to present subconsciously at the end of social interactions
and has a variety of meanings that must be taken in context. Its several
meanings include: I got caught, gleeful excitement, I got away with
something, I did something foolish, or I am naughty.

Just today, as I was going over some notes for this book, the attendant
at the university cafeteria placed the wrong vegetables on the plate of the
student directly in front of me. When the student spoke up to correct the
error, the attendant jutted her tongue out between her teeth and raised
her shoulders as if to say, "Oops, I made a mistake."

Fig. 82

Tongue jutting is seen when people get caught doing something they shouldn't, they screw up, or they are getting away with something. It is very brief.

In social or business discussions, this tongue-jut behavior is usually seen toward the end of the dialogue, when one person feels he has gotten away with something and the other party has failed to detect or pursue the matter. If you see tongue-jutting behavior, ask yourself what just transpired. Consider whether you may have been fooled or cheated, or that you or someone else just made a mistake. This is the time to assess whether someone is putting one over on you.

OTHER NONVERBAL BEHAVIORS OF THE FACE

Furrowed Forehead

Frowning, by furrowing the forehead (and brow), usually occurs when a person is anxious, sad, concentrating, concerned, bewildered, or angry (see figure 83). A forehead furrow needs to be examined in context to

Fig. 83

A furrowed forehead is an easy way to
assess for discomfort or anxiety. When
we are happy and content, you hardly see
this behavior.

determine its true meaning. For instance, I saw a supermarket cashier
closing out her register drawer, frowning as she went about counting her
cash. You could see the intensity and concentration of her expression, as
she tried to square the totals at the end of her shift. The same frown can
be observed in someone who has just been arrested and is being led out
past reporters. The furrowed forehead is usually present when someone
finds himself in an untenable or disagreeable situation but can't escape,
which is why you usually see it on arrest mug shots.

Incidentally, this frowning behavior is so ancient and so common to
mammals that even dogs will recognize it when we look at them with a
furrowed brow. Dogs themselves can exhibit a similar expression when
they are anxious, sad, or concentrating. Another interesting fact with regard to frowning is that as we get older and add to our life experiences,
our foreheads develop deeper and deeper furrows that eventually become
permanent wrinkles. Just as permanent smile lines may develop from a
lifetime of positive nonverbals and signify a happy life, a person with a

wrinkled brow likely has had a challenging life in which he engaged in frequent frowning.

Nasal Wing Dilation (Nose Flare)

As discussed previously, the flaring of nostrils is a facial cue that signals that a person is aroused. Lovers can often be seen hovering around each other, their nostrils subtly flaring in excitement and anticipation. Most likely, lovers engage in this subconscious behavior as they absorb each other's scents of sexual attraction known as *pheromones* (Givens, 2005, 191–208). Nose flaring is also an intention cue, a potent indicator of the intent to do something physical, and not necessarily sexual. It can be anything from getting ready to climb some steep stairs to preparing to move a bookcase. As people prepare to act physically, they will oxygenate, which causes the nostrils to flare.

As a law enforcement officer, if I encounter a person on the street looking down, his feet in the ready or "pugilistic position," with his nose flaring, I suspect that he is probably preparing to do one of three things: argue, run, or fight. Nasal wing dilation is something you should always be watching for if you are around someone who might have reason either to attack or run away from you. It is just one of many suspicious behaviors we should teach our children to watch for. That way they will be more aware when people are becoming dangerous, especially at school or on playgrounds.

Nail-Biting and Related Signs of Stress

If you see a person biting his nails while waiting to close a deal, he probably does not impress you as being very confident. Nail-biting is an indication of stress, insecurity, or discomfort. When you see it in a bargaining session, even if just for a moment, it is safe to assume that the nail-biter is unsure of himself and/or is bargaining from a position of weakness. People interviewing for jobs or young men waiting for their dates to arrive should avoid biting their nails, not only because it looks unsightly, but also because nail-biting shouts, "I am insecure." We bite our nails not because they need trimming primarily, but rather because it pacifies us.

Facial Blushing and Blanching

Sometimes we will involuntarily blush or blanch based on deep emotional states. To demonstrate blushing behavior in my classes, I will make a student stand in front of the group and then I will come up behind and get very close to the back of his or her neck. Usually this violation of the person's space will be enough to cause a limbic reaction, making the face blush. On some people, especially fair-skinned individuals, this can be very noticeable. People will also blush when they are caught doing something they know is wrong. Then there is the blushing that occurs when a person likes someone but doesn't want him or her to know it. Teenagers who harbor a secret crush on someone will often blush when that particular person draws near. This is a true limbic response that is transmitted by the body and is relatively easy to spot.

Conversely, blanching (turning pale) can take place when we are in the sustained limbic reaction known as shock. I have seen blanching as a result of a traffic accident or in an interview in which person was suddenly presented with overwhelming evidence of his guilt. Blanching takes place as the involuntary nervous system hijacks all the surface vessels and channels the blood to our larger muscles to prepare for escape or attack. I know of at least one case where an individual was so surprised to be arrested that he suddenly blanched and had a fatal heart attack. Although these behaviors are only skin deep, we should not ignore them, as they are indicative of high stress and will present differently according to the nature and the duration of the circumstances.

Disapproval Cues through Facial Expressions

Disapproval cues vary around the world and reflect a specific culture's social norms. In Russia, I have had people look at me with scorn because

I was whistling while walking down the hallway of an art museum. It seems that whistling indoors is a no-no in Russia. In Montevideo, I was among a group that was sanctioned with squinting eyes followed by a dismissive turn of the face away. Apparently our group was talking too loudly and locals did not appreciate our boisterous humor. In the United States, because the country is so large and diverse, different locales will have different disapproval displays; what you see in the Midwest is different from what you see in New England or New York.

Most disapproval displays show on the face and are among the earliest messages we learn from our parents and siblings. Those who care for us will give us "that face" to let us know if we are doing something wrong or getting out of line. My father, who is very stoic, had "the look" down pat; all he had to do was glance at me sternly and that was enough. It was a look that even my friends feared. The man never had to castigate us verbally. He just gave us that unmistakable glance, and that was it.

For the most part, we are fairly adept at understanding disapproval cues, although at times they can be very subtle (see box 55). Recognizing censure is a key to learning the unwritten rules and conventions of a country or area, as it conveys when we have broken them. These signals help us know when we are being rude. Undeserved and inappropriate displays of disapproval or censure, however, are likewise rude. One nonverbal of disapproval too commonly seen in America is rolling of the eyes. This is a sign of disrespect and must not be tolerated, especially from subordinates, staff, or children.

Facial displays of disgust or disapproval are very honest and are reflective of what is going on in the brain. Disgust likely registers primarily on the face because this is the part of our anatomy that was adapted, over millions of years, to reject spoiled food or anything else that might harm us. Although these facial displays may range from muted to obvious—whether confronted with negative or displeasing information or when tasting bad food—as far as the brain is concerned, the sentiment is the same. "I don't like this, get it away from me." No matter how slight the grimace or look of distaste or displeasure, we can be confident in interpreting these behaviors accurately because they are governed by the limbic system (see box 56).

BOX 55: **A WATERED-DOWN SALES PITCH**

Not long ago, I was approached by a saleswoman for a major chain of gyms in central Florida. The young lady was very enthusiastic to have me join the gym, stating it would only cost me a dollar a day for the rest of the year. As I listened, she became even more animated, as I think she saw me as a good prospect. When it was my turn to speak I asked if the gym had a pool. She said no, but that it had other great features. I then mentioned that currently I paid twenty-two dollars per month to attend my gym and that it had an Olympic-size pool. As I spoke, she looked down at her feet while making a microgesture of disgust (her nose and the left side of her mouth lifted upward) (see figure 84). It was a short and fleeting gesture, and if it had lasted longer, it would have looked like a snarl. This microgesture was enough for me to know that she was displeased with what I said, and after a second or two she made an excuse to leave me and approach someone else. Sales pitch over.

That was neither the first nor the last time I observed such behavior. In fact, I have often seen it in negotiations, where an offer is made and one of the participants involved suddenly and without conscious thought made a similar microgesture of disgust. When rejecting food being tendered in Latin America, it is very common to perform this behavior while shaking the head side to side, without saying a word. Interestingly, what is seen as rude in one setting or country may be a perfectly acceptable gesture in another. The key to successful travel is to know the customs in advance, so you know what to do and what to expect.

BOX 56: **TILL DISGUST DO US PART**

Just how accurate is this disgust gesture in revealing our inner thoughts and intentions? Here's a personal example. While I was visiting with a friend and his fiancée, he spoke of their upcoming marriage and honeymoon plans. Unbeknownst to him, I witnessed her make a facial micro-gesture of disgust as he uttered the word *marriage.* It was an extremely fleeting gesture, and I thought it odd since the topic appeared to be something about which both of them should have been excited. Months later, my friend called to tell me that his fiancée had backed out of the wedding. I had seen, in that single gesture, her brain registering its true sentiments without equivocation. The thought of going through with the marriage was repulsive to her.

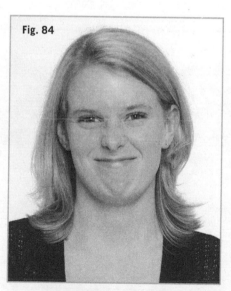

Fig. 84

We crinkle our noses to indicate dislike or disgust. This is very accurate but at times fleeting. In some cultures it is really pronounced.

GRAVITY-DEFYING BEHAVIORS OF THE FACE

The old adage "Keep your chin up" is a remark directed at someone who is in the doldrums or experiencing misfortune (see figures 85 and 86). This bit of folk wisdom accurately reflects our limbic response to adversity. A person with his chin down is seen as lacking confidence and experiencing negative sentiments while a person with his chin up is perceived as being in a positive frame of mind.

What is true with the chin is also true for the nose. A nose-up gravity-defying gesture is a high-confidence nonverbal tell, while a nose-down position is a display of low confidence. When people are stressed or upset, the chin (and nose, since it must follow along) tends not to be held high. Tucking the chin is a form of withdrawal or distancing and can be very accurate in discerning true negative sentiment.

In Europe, in particular, you see a lot more of these behaviors, especially holding the nose high when looking down on those of lower class or snubbing someone. I was watching French television while traveling

Fig. 85

When confidence is low or we are concerned for ourselves, the chin will tuck in, forcing the nose down.

Fig. 86

When we feel positive, the chin comes out and the nose is high: both signs of comfort and confidence.

abroad and noted how one politician, when asked a question he deemed beneath him, merely raised his nose high, looking down on the reporter, and answered "No, I will not answer that." The nose reflected his status and attitude of contempt for the reporter. Charles de Gaulle, a rather complex individual who eventually became the president of France, was famous for projecting this kind of haughty attitude and image.

The Rule of Mixed Signals

Sometimes we don't say what we're really thinking, but our faces reflect it anyway. For example, someone who is looking repeatedly at his watch or at the nearest exit is letting you know he is either running late, has an appointment, or would rather be elsewhere. This kind of look is an intention cue.

Other times, we say one thing but really believe otherwise. This brings us to a general rule when it comes to interpreting emotions and/ or words by looking at facial expressions. When confronted with mixed signals from the face (such as happiness cues along with anxiety signals or pleasure behaviors seen alongside displeasure displays), or if the verbal and nonverbal facial messages are not in agreement, always side with the negative emotion as the more honest of the two. The negative sentiment will almost always be the more accurate and genuine of the person's feelings and emotions. For instance, if someone says, "So happy to see you," with jaws tightened, the statement is false. The tension in the face reveals the true emotion the person is feeling. Why side with the negative emotion? Because our most immediate reaction to an objectionable situation is usually the most accurate; it is only after a moment when we realize that others might see us that we mask that initial response with some facial behavior that is more socially acceptable. So when confronted with both, go with the first emotion observed, especially if it is a negative emotion.

CONCLUDING THOUGHTS ON THE FACE

Because the face can convey so many different expressions and because we are taught to mask our facial displays at an early age, anything you observe on the face should be compared with the nonverbals of the rest of the body. In addition, because facial-cue behaviors are so complex, it may be difficult to interpret whether they reflect comfort or discomfort. If you are confused as to the meaning of a facial expression, reenact it and sense how it makes you feel. You will find this little trick may help you decipher what you just observed. The face can reveal a great deal of information but it can also mislead. You need to look for clusters of behaviors, constantly evaluate what you see in its context, and note whether the facial expression agrees with—or is in contrast to—signals from other parts of the body. Only by performing all of these observations can you confidently validate your assessment of a person's emotions and intentions.

EIGHT

Detecting Deception

Proceed with Caution!

Throughout the book, we've touched on many examples of nonverbal behavior, the body signals we can utilize to better understand the feelings, thoughts, and intentions of others. By now, I hope you have been persuaded that with these nonverbal clues, you can accurately assess what every *body* is saying, in any setting. There is, however, one type of human behavior that is difficult to read, and that is deception.

You might assume that as a career FBI agent who has at times been called a human lie detector, I can spot deceit with relative ease, and even teach you to become a personal polygraph in short order. Nothing could be further from the truth! In reality, it is extremely difficult to detect deception—far more so than getting an accurate read on the other behaviors we have discussed throughout this book.

It is precisely because of my experience as an FBI agent involved in behavioral analysis—a person who has spent his entire career attempting to detect lies—that I recognize and appreciate the difficulties in accurately assessing deceptive behavior. It is also for that reason that I have chosen to devote an entire chapter—and to end this book—with a *realistic* appraisal and application of nonverbal behaviors in detecting deception. Lots of books have been written on this subject that make it sound easy, even for amateurs. I assure you, it is not!

I believe this is the first time a career law enforcement and counterintelligence officer with a considerable background in this field, and who still teaches in the intelligence community, has stepped forward to sound this warning: most people—both laypersons and professionals—are not very good at detecting lies. Why make this statement? Because, unfortunately, I have seen too many investigators misinterpret nonverbal behaviors over the years, making innocent people feel culpable or unnecessarily uncomfortable. I have also seen both amateurs and professionals make claims that are outrageous, ruining lives in the process. Too many people have gone to jail for giving false confessions just because an officer mistook a stress response for a lie. Newspapers are replete with horror stories, including the one about the New York Central Park jogger, wherein officers mistook nonverbals of stress for deception and pressured the innocent into confessions (Kassin, 2004, 172–194; Kassin, 2006, 207–227). It is my hope that readers of this book will have a more realistic and honest picture of what can and cannot be achieved through the nonverbal approach to detecting deception, and, armed with this knowledge, they will take a more reasoned, cautious approach to declaring when a person is or is not telling the truth.

DECEPTION: A TOPIC WORTHY OF STUDY

We all have a stake in the truth. Society functions based on an assumption that people will abide by their word—that truth prevails over mendacity. For the most part, it does. If it didn't, relationships would have a short shelf life, commerce would cease, and trust between parents and children would be destroyed. All of us depend on honesty, because when truth is lacking we suffer, and society suffers. When Adolf Hitler lied to Neville Chamberlain, there was not peace in our time, and over fifty million people paid the price with their lives. When Richard Nixon lied to the nation, it destroyed the respect many had for the office of the president. When Enron executives lied to their employees, thousands of lives were ruined overnight. We count on our government and commercial institutions to be honest and truthful. We need and expect our friends and family to be truthful. Truth is essential for all relations be they personal, professional, or civic.

We are fortunate that, for the most part, people are honest and that most of the lies we hear daily are actually social or "white" lies, meant to protect us from the true answer to questions such as "Do I look fat in this outfit?" Unquestionably, when it comes to more serious matters, it is in our own self-interest to assess and determine the truth of what we are told. Achieving this, however, is not easy. For thousands of years, people have been using soothsayers and all manner of dubious techniques— such as putting a hot knife on a person's tongue—to detect deception. Even today, some organizations use handwriting samples, voice-stress analysis, or the polygraph to spot liars. All of these methods have questionable results. There is no method, no machine, no test, no person that is 100 percent accurate at uncovering deception. Even the vaunted polygraph is accurate only 60 to 80 percent of the time, depending on the operator of the instrument (Ford, 1996, 230–232; Cumming, 2007).

Looking For Liars

The truth is that identifying deceit is so difficult that repeated studies begun in the 1980s show that most of us—including judges, attorneys, clinicians, police officers, FBI agents, politicians, teachers, mothers, fathers, and spouses—are no better than chance (fifty-fifty) when it comes to detecting deception (Ford, 1996, 217, Ekman, 1991, 162). It is disturbing but true. Most people, including professionals, do no better than a coin toss at correctly perceiving dishonesty (Ekman & O'Sullivan,

1991, 913–920). Even those who are truly gifted at detecting deception (probably less than 1 percent of the general population) seldom are right more than 60 percent of the time. Consider the countless jurors who must determine honesty or dishonesty, guilt or innocence, based on what they think are deceptive behaviors. Unfortunately, those behaviors most often mistaken for dishonesty are primarily manifestations of stress, not deception (Ekman, 1991, 187–188). That's why I live by the motto taught to me by those who know that there is no single behavior that is indicative of deception—not one (Ekman, 1991, 162–189).

This does not mean that we should abandon our efforts to study deception and observe for behaviors that, in context, are suggestive of it. My advice is to set a realistic goal: to be able to read nonverbal behaviors with clarity and reliability, and let the human body speak to you as to what it is thinking, feeling, or intending. These are more reasonable objectives that, in the end, will not only help you understand others more effectively (lying isn't the only behavior worth detecting!), but will also give you clues to deception as a byproduct of your observations.

What Makes Deception So Difficult to Detect?

If you're wondering why identifying deception is so difficult, consider the old adage "Practice makes perfect." We learn to lie at such an early age—and we do it so often—that we become skillful at telling falsehoods convincingly. To illustrate, think of how often you have heard something like, "Tell them we are not home," or "Put on a party smile," or "Don't tell your dad what happened or we'll both be in trouble." Because we are social animals, we not only lie for our own benefit, but we lie for the benefit of each other (Vrij, 2003, 3–11). Lying can be a way to avoid giving a lengthy explanation, an attempt to avoid punishment, a shortcut to a bogus doctoral degree, or it can simply be used to be nice. Even our cosmetics and padded clothing help us to deceive. In essence, for us humans, lying is a "tool for social survival" (St-Yves, 2007).

A NEW APPROACH TO UNCOVERING DECEPTION

During my last year at the FBI, I submitted my research and findings on deception, including a review of the literature for the previous forty years. This led to the FBI publication of an article entitled "A Four-Domain Model of Detecting Deception: An Alternative Paradigm for Interviewing" (Navarro, 2003, 19–24). This paper presented a new model for identifying dishonesty based on the concept of limbic arousal and our displays of comfort and discomfort, or the *comfort/discomfort domain*. Simply put, I suggested that when we are telling the truth and have no worries, we tend to be more comfortable than when we are lying or concerned about getting caught because we harbor "guilty knowledge." The model also shows how we tend to display more emphatic behaviors when we are comfortable and truthful, and when we are uncomfortable, we don't.

This model is currently being used worldwide. Although its purpose was to train law enforcement officers to detect deception during criminal investigations, it is applicable to any type of interpersonal interaction—at work, at home, or anywhere in which differentiating dishonesty from truth is important. As I present it to you here, you'll be uniquely prepared to understand it because of what you have learned in previous chapters.

The Critical Role of the Comfort/Discomfort Equation in Detecting Deception

Those who are lying or are guilty and must carry the knowledge of their lies and/or crimes with them find it difficult to achieve comfort, and their tension and distress may be readily observed. Attempting to disguise their guilt or deception places a very distressing cognitive load on them as they struggle to fabricate answers to what would otherwise be simple questions (DePaulo et al., 1985, 323–370).

The more comfortable a person is when speaking with us, the easier it will be to detect the critical nonverbals of discomfort associated with deception. Your goal is to establish high comfort during the early part of any interaction or during "rapport building." This helps you to establish a baseline of behaviors during that period when the person, hopefully, does not feel threatened.

Establishing a Comfort Zone for Detecting Deception

In pursuing the detection of deception, you must realize *your* impact on the actions of a suspected liar, and recognize that how you behave will affect the other person's behavior (Ekman, 1991, 170–173). How you ask the questions (accusingly), how you sit (too close), how you look upon the person (suspiciously), will either support or disrupt their comfort level. It is well established that if you violate people's space, if you act suspicious, if you look at them the wrong way, or ask questions with a prosecutorial tone, it negatively intrudes on the interview. First and foremost, unmasking liars is not about identifying dishonesty, but rather it is about how you observe and question others in order to detect deception. Then, it is about the collection of nonverbal intelligence. The more you see (clusters of behavior), the more confidence you can have in your observations, and the greater your chances for perceiving when someone is being untruthful.

Even if you are actively looking for deception during a discussion or interview, your role should be *neutral*, to the extent possible, not suspicious. Remember that the moment you become suspicious, you are affecting how a person will respond to you. If you say, "You are lying" or "I think you are not telling the truth," or even simply look at him or her suspiciously, you will influence the person's behaviors (Vrij, 2003, 67). The best way to proceed is just to ask for ever-more clarifying details about the matter, such as a simple "I don't understand" or "Can you explain how that happened again?" Often merely getting someone to expand on his or her statement will suffice in eventually sorting deceit from truth. Whether you are attempting to ascertain the validity of someone's credentials during an employment interview, the truth about a theft at work, or especially if you are engaged in a serious discussion regarding finances or potential infidelity with your spouse, keeping your cool is essential. Try to remain calm as you ask questions, don't act suspicious, and appear comfortable and nonjudgmental. That way the person you are speaking with will be less likely to be defensive and/or unwilling to divulge information.

Defining Signs of Comfort

Comfort is readily apparent in conversations with family and friends. We sense when people are having a good time and are comfortable in our presence. While seated at a table, people who are comfortable with each other will move objects aside so that nothing blocks their view. Over time, they may draw closer so they do not have to talk as loudly. Individuals who are comfortable display their bodies more openly, showing more of their torsos and the insides of their arms and legs (they allow ventral access or fronting). In the presence of strangers, comfort is more difficult to achieve, especially in stressful situations such as a formal interview or a deposition. That is why it's so important that you do your best to create a comfort zone from the very outset of your interaction with another individual.

When we are comfortable, there should be *synchrony* in our nonverbal behavior. The breathing rhythm of two comfortable people will be similar, as will the tone and pitch of their speech and their general demeanor. Just think of a couple leaning toward each other at a café as they sit in full comfort. If one leans forward, the other follows, the phenomenon known as isopraxism. If a person is standing while talking to us, leaning to the side with hands in the pockets and feet crossed, most likely we will do the same (see figure 87). By mirroring another person's behavior, we are subconsciously saying, "I am comfortable with you."

In an interview setting or any situation where a difficult topic is being discussed, the tone of each party should mirror the other over time if there is synchrony (Cialdini, 1993, 167–207). If harmony does not exist between the people involved, this synchrony will be missing and discernible. They may sit differently, talk in a manner or tone different from

Fig. 87

Here is an example of isopraxis: Both people are
mirroring each other and leaning toward each
other, showing signs of high comfort.

each other, or at the least their expressions will be at odds, if not totally
disparate. Asynchrony is a barrier to effective communication and is a
serious obstacle to a successful interview or discussion.

If you are relaxed and poised during a conversation or interview,
while the other party continually looks at the clock or sits in a way that is
tense or lacks movement (referred to as *flash frozen*), this is suggestive that
there is no comfort, even though to the untrained eye it may appear that
everything is all right (Knapp & Hall, 2002, 321; Schafer & Navarro,
2004, 66). If the other person seeks disruptions or talks repeatedly of fi-
nalizing the conversation, these too are signs of discomfort.

Obviously, displays of comfort are more common in people speaking the truth; there is no stress to conceal, and no guilty knowledge to make them uncomfortable (Ekman, 1991, 185). Thus, you should be looking for signs of discomfort—when they occur and in what context—to assess for possible deception.

Signs of Discomfort in an Interaction

We show discomfort when we do not like what is happening to us, when we do not like what we are seeing or hearing, or when we are compelled to talk about things we would prefer to keep hidden. We display discomfort first in our physiology, due to arousal of the limbic brain. Our heart rate quickens, our hairs stand on end, we perspire more, and we breathe faster. Beyond the physiological responses, which are autonomic (automatic) and require no thinking on our part, our bodies manifest discomfort nonverbally. We tend to move our bodies in an attempt to block or distance, we rearrange ourselves, jiggle our feet, fidget, twist at the hips, or drum our fingers when we are scared, nervous, or significantly uncomfortable (de Becker, 1997, 133). We have all noticed such discomfort behaviors in others—whether at a job interview, on a date, or when being questioned about a serious matter at work or home. Remember that these actions do not automatically indicate deception; however, they do indicate that a person is uncomfortable in the current situation for any number of reasons.

If you are attempting to observe discomfort as a potential indicator of deception, the best setting is one that has no objects (such as furniture, tables, desks, or chairs) between you and the person you are observing or interviewing. Because we have noted that the lower limbs are particularly honest, if the person is behind a desk or table, try to move it or convene away from it, as such an obstacle will block the vast majority (nearly 80 percent) of the body surfaces that should be observed. In fact, watch for liars to use obstacles or objects (such as a pillow, a drinking glass, or a chair) to form a barrier between you and them (see box 57). The use of objects is a sign that an individual wants distance, separation, and partial concealment, because he or she is being

---

BOX 57: **BUILDING THE WALL**

In my role with the FBI years ago, I conducted a joint interview of a subject along with an officer from a fellow law enforcement agency. During
the interview, a very uncomfortable and dishonest man gradually built a
barrier in front of himself using soda cans, pencil holders, and various
documents that were on the desk of my interviewing partner. He ultimately planted a backpack on the table between himself and the interviewers. The building of this barrier was so gradual that we did not realize
it until we later looked at the video. This nonverbal behavior occurred
because the subject was attempting to derive comfort by hiding behind a
wall of materials, thus distancing himself. Obviously, we got little information or cooperation, and for the most part, he lied.

---

less open—which goes hand in hand with being uncomfortable or
even deceitful.

Incidentally, when it comes to interviewing, or any conversation in
which you are interested in ascertaining the truth or genuineness of a
person's statements, you may gain more nonverbal information if you are
standing; you can pick up on a lot of behaviors standing that simply go
unnoticed while sitting. While a lengthy period of standing may be impractical or unnatural in some settings, such as at a formal job interview,
there are often still opportunities to observe standing behaviors, such as
when greeting or conversing while waiting for a table at lunch.

When we are uncomfortable with those around us, we tend to distance ourselves from them. This is especially true of individuals trying
to deceive us. Even while sitting side by side, we will lean away from
those with whom we feel uncomfortable, often moving either our torsos
or our feet away or toward an exit. These behaviors can occur during
conversations either because of the difficult, unnerving, or sour relationship between the parties involved or because of the subject matter being
discussed.

Other clear signs of discomfort seen in people during a difficult or troubling conversation include rubbing the forehead near the temple region, squeezing the face, rubbing the neck, or stroking the back of the head with the hand. People may show their displeasure by rolling their eyes in disrespect, picking lint off themselves (preening), or talking down to the person asking the questions—giving short answers, becoming resistant, hostile, or sarcastic, or even displaying microgestures with indecent connotations such as giving the finger (Ekman, 1991, 101–103). Envision a snotty and indignant teenager who is being questioned about a new and expensive sweater her mother suspects was stolen from the mall and you'll have a clear idea of all the defensive maneuvers an uncomfortable person can display.

When making false statements, liars will rarely touch or engage in other physical contact with you. I found this to be particularly true of informants who had gone bad and were giving false information for money. Since touching is more often performed by the truthful person for emphasis, this distancing helps to alleviate the level of anxiety a dishonest person is feeling. Any diminution of touching observed in a person engaged in conversation, especially while hearing or answering critical questions, is more likely than not to be indicative of deception (Lieberman, 1998, 24). If possible and appropriate, you may consider sitting close to a loved one when questioning him or her about something serious, or even holding your child's hand while you discuss a difficult matter. In this way you may more readily note changes in touch throughout the conversation.

A failure to touch does not automatically indicate someone is deceptive, however, and physical contact is clearly more appropriate and expected in some of our interpersonal relationships than others. It is true that a lack of touch may signify that someone does not like you, since we also don't touch those we don't respect or for whom we have contempt. The bottom line is that assessing the nature and length of the relationship is also important in discerning the meaning of such distancing behavior.

When looking at the face for signs of comfort or discomfort, look for subtle behaviors such as a grimace or a look of contempt (Ekman, 1991, 158–169). Also watch for a person's mouth to quiver or squirm in discomfort during a serious discussion. Any facial expression that lasts too long or lingers is not normal, whether a smile, a frown, or a surprised look. Such contrived behavior during a conversation or an interview is intended to influence opinion and lacks authenticity. Often when people are caught doing something wrong or lying, they will hold a smile for what seems an eternity. Rather than indicating comfort, this type of false smile is actually a discomfort display.

When we do not like something we hear, whether a question or an answer, we often close our eyes as if to block out what was just heard. The various forms of eye-blocking mechanisms are analogous to folding our hands tightly across our chest or turning away from those with whom we disagree. These blocking displays are performed subconsciously and occur often, especially during a formal interview, and are usually related to a specific topic. Eyelid flutter is also observed at times when a particular subject causes distress (Navarro & Schafer, 2001, 10).

All of these eye manifestations are powerful clues as to how information is registering or what questions are problematic for the recipient. However, they are not necessarily direct indicators of deceit. Little or no eye contact is *not* indicative of deception (Vrij, 2003, 38–39). This is rubbish for reasons discussed in the previous chapter.

Keep in mind that predators and habitual liars actually engage in greater eye contact than most individuals, and will lock eyes with you. Research clearly shows that Machiavellian people (for example, psychopaths, con men, and habitual liars) will actually increase eye contact during deception (Ekman, 1991, 141–142). Perhaps this increase in eye contact is consciously employed by such individuals because it is so commonly (but erroneously) believed that looking someone straight in the eye is a sign of truthfulness.

Be aware that there are cultural differences in eye contact and eye-gaze behavior that must be considered in any attempt to detect deception. For example, individuals belonging to certain groups of people (African Americans and Latin Americans, for instance) may be taught to look down or away from parental authority out of respect when questioned or being scolded (Johnson, 2007, 280–281).

Take note of the head movements of those with whom you are speaking. If a person's head begins to shake either in the affirmative or in the negative as he is speaking, and the movement occurs simultaneously with what he is saying, then the statement can typically be relied upon as being truthful. If, however, the head shake or head movement is delayed or occurs after the speech, then most likely the statement is contrived and not truthful. Although it may be very subtle, the delayed movement of the head is an attempt to further validate what has been stated and is not part of the natural flow of communication. In addition, honest head movements should be consistent with verbal denials or affirmations. If a head movement is inconsistent with or contrary to a person's statement, it may indicate deception. While typically involving more subtle than exaggerated head movements, this incongruity of verbal and nonverbal signals happens more often than we think. For example, someone may say, "I didn't do it," while his head is slightly nodding in the affirmative.

During discomfort, the limbic brain takes over, and a person's face can conversely either flush or lighten in color. During difficult conversations, you may also see increased perspiration or breathing; note whether the person is noticeably wiping off sweat or trying to control his or her breathing in an effort to remain calm. Any trembling of the body, whether of the hands, fingers, or lips, or any attempt to hide or restrain the hands or lips (through disappearing or compressed lips), may be indicative of discomfort and/or deception, especially if it occurs after normal nervousness should have worn off.

A person's voice may crack or may seem inconsistent during deceptive speech; swallowing becomes difficult as the throat becomes dry from stress, so look for hard swallows. These can be evidenced by a sudden bob or jump of the Adam's apple and may be accompanied by the clearing or repeated clearings of the throat—all indicative of discomfort. Keep in mind that these behaviors are indicators of distress, not guarantees of deception. I have seen very honest people testify in court displaying all these behaviors simply because they were nervous, not because they were lying. Even after years of testifying in federal and state courts,

I still get nervous when I am on the stand, so signs of tension and stress always need to be deciphered in context.

Pacifiers and Discomfort

When interviewing suspects during my years with the FBI, I looked for pacifying behaviors to help guide me in my questioning and to assess what was particularly stressful to the interviewee. Although pacifiers alone are not definitive proof of deception (since they can manifest in innocent people who are nervous), they do provide another piece of the puzzle in determining what a person is truly thinking and feeling.

The following is a list of twelve things I do—and the points I keep in mind—when I want to read pacifying nonverbals in interpersonal interactions. You might consider using a similar strategy when you interview or converse with others, be it a formal inquiry, a serious conversation with a family member, or an interaction with a business associate.

(1) Get a clear view. When I conduct interviews or interact with others, I don't want anything blocking my total view of the person, as I don't want to miss any pacifying behaviors. If, for example, the person pacifies by wiping his hands on his lap, I want to be able to see it—which is difficult if there is a desk in the way. Human resource personnel should be aware that the best way to interview is in a physically open space—with nothing blocking your view of the candidate—so you may fully observe the person you are interviewing.

(2) Expect some pacifying behaviors. A certain level of pacifying behavior is normal in everyday nonverbal displays; people do this to calm themselves. When my daughter was young, she would soothe herself to sleep by playing with her hair, curling the strands in her fingers, seemingly oblivious to the world. So I expect people to pacify more or less, throughout the day, just as I expect them to breathe, as they adapt to an ever-changing environment.

(3) Expect initial nervousness. Initial nervousness in an interview or serious conversation is normal, particularly when circumstances surrounding the meeting are stressful. For example, a father asking his son about his homework assignment will not be as stressful as asking the boy why he was expelled from school for disruptive behavior.

(4) Get the person with whom you're interacting to relax first. As an interview, important meeting, or significant discussion progresses, eventually those involved should calm down and become more comfortable. In fact, a good interviewer will make sure this happens by taking time to let the person become more relaxed before asking questions or exploring topics that might be stressful.

(5) Establish a baseline. Once a person's pacifying behaviors have decreased and stabilized to normal (for that person), the interviewer can use that pacifying level as a baseline for assessing future behavior.

(6) Look for increased use of pacifiers. As the interview or conversation continues, you should be observant of pacifying behaviors and/or an increase (spike) in their frequency, particularly when they occur in response to a specific question or piece of information. Such an increase is a clue that something about the question or information has troubled the person pacifying, and that topic likely deserves further attention and focus. It is important to identify correctly the specific stimulus (whether a question, information, or event) that caused the pacifying response; otherwise you might draw the wrong conclusions or move the discussion in the wrong direction. For example, if during an employment interview the candidate starts to ventilate his shirt collar (a pacifier) when asked a certain question about his former position, that specific inquiry has caused sufficient stress that his brain is requiring pacification. This indicates the issue needs to be pursued further. The behavior does not necessarily mean that deception is involved, but simply that the topic is causing the interviewee stress.

(7) Ask, pause, and observe. Good interviewers, like good conversationalists, do not machine gun questions by firing one right after the other in a staccato fashion. You will be hard-pressed to detect deception accurately if your impatience or impertinence antagonizes the person with whom you are speaking. Ask a question and then wait to observe all the reactions. Give the interviewee time to think and respond, and build in pregnant pauses to achieve this objective. Also, questions should be crafted in such a way as to elicit specific answers in order to better zero in on facts and fiction. The more specific the question, the more likely you are to elicit precise nonverbals, and now that you have better understanding of the meaning of subconscious actions, the more accurate your assessments will be. In law enforcement interviews, unfortunately, many false confessions have been obtained through sustained staccato-like questioning, which causes high stress and obfuscates nonverbal cues. We now know that innocent people will confess to crimes, and even give written statements, in order to terminate a stressful interview wherein pressure is applied (Kassin, 2006, 207–228). The same holds true for sons, daughters, spouses, friends, and employees when grilled by an overzealous person, be it a parent, husband, wife, companion, or boss.

(8) Keep the person you are interviewing focused. Interviewers should keep in mind that many times when people are simply talking—when they are telling their side of the story—there will be fewer useful nonverbals performed than when the interviewer controls the scope of the topic. Pointed questions elicit behavioral manifestations that are useful in assessing a person's honesty.

(9) Chatter is not truth. One mistake made by both novice and experienced interviewers is the tendency to equate talking with truth. When interviewees are talking, we tend to believe them; when they are reserved, we assume they are lying. During conversation, people who provide an overwhelming

---

BOX 58: **IT'S ALL A LIE**

I remember one case in which I interviewed a woman in Macon, Georgia. For three days she voluntarily provided us with page after page of information. I really felt we were on to something when the interview was finally over, until it came time to corroborate what this woman had said. For over a year we investigated her claims (both in the United States and in Europe), but in the end, after expending significant effort and resources, we discovered that everything she had told us was a lie. She had provided us pages and pages of plausible lies, even implicating her innocent husband. Had I remembered that cooperation does not always equal truth, and had I scrutinized her more carefully, we would have been spared wasting a great deal of time and money. The information this woman had given sounded good and seemed plausible, but it was all trash. I wish I could say this incident happened to me early in my career, but it did not. I am neither the first—nor will I be the last—interviewer to be bamboozled this way. Though some people naturally talk more than others, you should always be on the lookout for this kind of chatty ploy.

---

amount of information and detail about an event or situation may appear to be telling the truth; however, they may be presenting a fabricated smoke screen they hope will obfuscate the facts or lead the conversation in another direction. The truth is revealed *not in the volume* of material spoken but *through the verification of facts* provided by the speaker. Until the information is verified, it is self-reported and perhaps meaningless data (see box 58).

(10) Stress coming in and going out. Based on years of studying interviewee behavior, I have concluded that a person with guilty knowledge will present two distinct behavior patterns, in sequence, when asked a difficult question such as, "Did you ever go inside the home of Mr. Jones?" The first behavior will

reflect the stress experienced when hearing the question. The interviewee will subconsciously respond with various distancing behaviors including foot withdrawal (moving them away from the investigator); he may lean away or may tighten his jaw and lips. This will be followed by the second set of related behaviors, pacifying responses to the stress that may include signals such as neck touching, nose stroking, or neck massaging as he ponders the question or answer.

(11) Isolate the cause of the stress. Two behavior patterns in series— the stress indicators followed by pacifying behaviors—have traditionally been erroneously associated with deception. This is unfortunate, because these manifestations need to be explained more simply as what they are—indicators of stress and stress relief—not necessarily dishonesty. No doubt someone who is lying may display these same behaviors, but individuals who are nervous also show them. Occasionally I will hear someone say, "If people talk while touching their nose, they are lying." It may be true that people who are deceptive touch their nose while speaking, but so do individuals who are honest but under stress. The nose touching is a pacifying behavior to relieve internal tension—regardless of the source of that discomfort. Even a retired FBI agent who is stopped for speeding with no legitimate explanation will touch his nose when pulled over (yes, I paid the ticket). My point is this. Don't be so hasty to assume deception when you see someone touching his or her nose. For everyone who does it while lying, you will find a hundred who do it out of habit to relieve stress.

(12) Pacifiers say so much. By helping us identify when a person is stressed, pacifying behaviors help us identify issues that need further focus and exploration. Through effective questioning we can both elicit and identify these pacifiers in *any* interpersonal interaction to achieve a better understanding of a person's thoughts and intentions.

TWO PRINCIPAL NONVERBAL BEHAVIORAL PATTERNS TO CONSIDER IN DETECTING DECEPTION

When it comes to body signals that alert us to the possibility of deception, you should be watching for nonverbal behaviors involving synchrony and emphasis.

Synchrony

Earlier in this chapter, I discussed the importance of synchrony as a way to assess for comfort in interpersonal interaction. Synchrony is also important, however, in assessing for deception. Look for synchrony between what is being said verbally and nonverbally, between the circumstances of the moment and what the subject is saying, between events and emotions, and even synchrony of time and space.

When being questioned, a person answering in the affirmative should have congruent head movement that immediately supports what is said; it should not be delayed. Lack of synchrony is exhibited when a person states, "I did not do it," while her head is nodding in an affirmative motion. Likewise, asynchrony is demonstrated when a man is asked, "Would you lie about this?" and his head gives a slight nod while he answers, "No." Upon catching themselves in this faux pas, people will reverse their head movements in an attempt to do damage control. When asynchronous behavior is observed, it looks contrived and pathetic. More often a mendacious statement, such as an untruthful "I did not do it," is followed by a noticeably delayed and less emphatic negative head movement. These behaviors are not synchronous and therefore more likely to be equated with deception because they show discomfort in their production.

There should also be synchrony between what is being said and the events of the moment. For instance, when parents are reporting the alleged kidnapping of their infant, there should be synchrony between the event (kidnapping) and their emotions. The distraught mother and father should be clamoring for law enforcement assistance, emphasizing every detail, feeling the depths of despair, eager to help, and willing to tell and retell the story, even at personal risk. When such reports are made by placid individuals, more concerned with getting one particular version of the story out and lacking in consistent emotional displays, or who are more concerned about their own well-being and how they are perceived, it is behavior that is totally out of synchrony with circumstances and inconsistent with honesty.

Lastly, there should be synchrony between events, time, and place. A person who delays reporting a significant event, such as the drowning of a friend, spouse, or child, or who travels to another jurisdiction to report the event should rightfully come under suspicion. Furthermore, the reporting of events that would have been impossible to observe from the person's vantage point is asynchronous, and therefore suspect. People who lie do not consider how synchrony fits into the equation, and their nonverbals and stories will eventually fail them. Achieving synchrony is a form of comfort and, as we have seen, plays a major role during police interviews and the reporting of crimes; but it will also set the stage for successful and meaningful conversations about all manner of serious issues in which detecting deceit is important.

Emphasis

When we speak, we naturally utilize various parts of our body—such as the eyebrows, head, hands, arms, torso, legs, and feet—to emphasize a point about which we feel deeply or emotionally. Observing emphasis is important because emphasis is universal when people are being genuine. Emphasis is the limbic brain's contribution to communication, a way to let others know just how potently we feel. Conversely, when the limbic brain does not back up what we say, we emphasize less or not at all. For the most part, in my experience and that of others, liars do not emphasize (Lieberman, 1998, 37). Liars will engage their cognitive brains in order to decide what to say and how to deceive, but rarely do they think about the presentation of the lie. When compelled to lie, most people are not aware of how much emphasis or accentuation enters into everyday conversations. When liars attempt to fabricate an answer, their emphasis looks unnatural or is delayed; rarely do they emphasize where appropriate, or they choose to do so only on relatively unimportant matters.

We emphasize both verbally and nonverbally. Verbally, we emphasize through voice, pitch, or tone, or through repetition. We also emphasize nonverbally, and these behaviors can be even more accurate and useful than words when attempting to detect the truth or dishonesty in a conversation or interview. People who typically use their hands while speaking punctuate their remarks with hand gestures, even going so far as pounding on a desk as they emphasize. Other individuals accentuate with the tips of the fingers by either gesturing with them or touching things. Hand behaviors complement honest speech, thoughts, and true sentiments (Knapp & Hall, 2002, 277–284). Raising our eyebrows (eyebrow flash) and widening our eyes are also ways of emphasizing a point (Morris, 1985, 61; Knapp & Hall, 2002, 68).

Another manifestation of emphasis is seen when someone leans forward with the torso, showing interest. We employ gravity-defying gestures such as rising up on the balls of our feet when we make a significant or emotionally charged point. When seated, people emphasize by raising the knee (staccato-like) while highlighting important points, and added emphasis can be shown by slapping the knee as it comes up, indicating emotional exuberance. Gravity-defying gestures are emblematic of emphasis and true sentiment, something liars rarely display.

In contrast, people de-emphasize or show lack of commitment to their own speech by speaking behind their hands (talking while covering their mouths) or showing limited facial expression. People control their countenance and engage in other movement restriction and withdrawal behaviors when they are not committed to what they are saying (Knapp & Hall, 2002, 320; Lieberman, 1998, 37). Deceptive people often show deliberative, pensive displays, such as fingers to the chin or stroking of cheeks, as though they are still thinking about what to say; this is in stark contrast to honest people who emphasize the point they are making. Deceptive people spend time evaluating what they say and how it is being received, which is inconsistent with honest behavior.

SPECIFIC NONVERBAL BEHAVIORS TO CONSIDER IN DETECTING DECEPTION

Below are some specific things you'll want to watch for when examining emphasis as a means for detecting possible deception.

Lack of Emphasis in Hand Behaviors

As Aldert Vrij and others have reported, lack of arm movement and lack of emphasis are suggestive of deception. The problem is there is no way of measuring this, especially in a public or social setting. Nevertheless, strive to note when it occurs and in what context, especially if it comes after a significant topic is brought up (Vrij, 2003, 25–27). Any sudden change in movement reflects brain activity. When arms shift from being animated to being still, there must be a reason, be it dejection or (possibly) deception.

In my own interviewing experiences, I have noticed that liars will tend to display less steepling. I also look for the white knuckles of the individual who grabs the chair armrest in a fixed manner as though in an "ejector seat." Unfortunately, for this uncomfortable person, ejection from the discussion is often impossible. Many criminal investigators have found that when the head, neck, arms, and legs are held in place with little movement and the hands and arms are clutching the armrest, such behavior is very much consistent with those who are about to deceive, but again, it is not definitive (Schafer & Navarro, 2003, 66) (see figure 88).

Interestingly, as individuals make declarative statements that are false, they will avoid touching not only other people, but objects such as a podium or table as well. I have never seen or heard a person who is lying yell affirmatively, "I didn't do it," while pounding his fist on the table. Usually what I have seen are very weak, nonemphatic statements, with gestures that are equally mild. People who are being deceptive lack commitment and confidence in what they are saying. Although their thinking brain (neocortex) will decide what to say in order to mislead, their

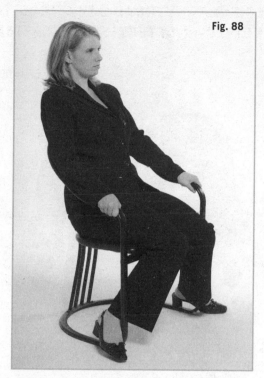

Fig. 88

Sitting for long periods in a chair, as though
flash frozen in an ejector seat, is evidence of
high stress and discomfort.

emotive brain (the limbic system—the honest part of the brain) simply
will not be committed to the ruse, and therefore will not emphasize their
statements using nonverbal behaviors (such as gestures). The sentiments
of the limbic brain are hard to override. Try to smile fully at someone
you dislike. It is extremely difficult to do. As with a false or fake smile,
false statements come with weak or passive nonverbals.

The Rogatory Position

When a person places his outstretched arms in front of his body, with
palms up, this is known as the *rogatory* (or "prayerful") display (see figure
89). Those who worship will turn their palms up to God to ask for
mercy. Likewise, captured soldiers will turn up their palms as they

Fig. 89

The palms-up or "rogatory" position usually indicates the person wants to be believed or wants to be accepted. It is not a dominant, confident display.

approach their captors. This behavior is also seen in individuals who say something when they want you to believe them. During a discussion, observe the person with whom you are speaking. When she makes a declarative statement, note whether her hands are palm up or palm down. During regular conversation in which ideas are being discussed and neither party is vehemently committed to a particular point, I expect to see both palm-up and palm-down displays.

However, when a person is making a passionate and assertive declaration such as, "You have to believe me, I did not kill her," those hands should be face down (see figure 90). If the statement is made palms up, the individual supplicating to be believed, I would find such a statement highly suspect. While this is not definitive, I would question any declarative statement made with the palms up. The palm-up position is not very affirmative and suggests that the person is asking to be believed. The

Fig. 90

Statements made palm down are more emphatic and more confident than statements made with hands palm up in the rogatory position.

truthful don't have to plead to be believed; they make a statement and it stands.

Territorial Displays and Deception

When we are confident and comfortable, we spread out. When we are less secure, we tend to take up less space. In extreme circumstances, distressed people may fold their arms and legs into their own body, assuming an almost fetal position. Uncomfortable conversations and interviews can evoke a variety of withdrawn postures: arms that are intertwined like a pretzel and/or ankles that are locked in place, sometimes to the point of being almost painful to the observer. Look especially for dramatic changes in body position that could be indicative of deception, particularly when they occur concurrently with a specific change of topic.

When we are confident about what we believe or what we are saying, we tend to sit up, with shoulders and back wide, exhibiting an erect posture indicative of security. When people are being deceitful or are outright lying, they subconsciously tend to stoop or sink into the furniture as if they are attempting to escape what is being said—even if they, themselves, are saying it. Those who are insecure, or are unsure of themselves, their thoughts, or their beliefs, are likely to reflect this in their posture—usually by stooping slightly, but sometimes dramatically by lowering their heads and drawing the shoulders up to the ears. Look for this "turtle effect" whenever people are uncomfortable and are trying to hide in the open. It is definitely a display of insecurity and discomfort.

Shoulder Shrugs

Although we all shrug at one time or another when we are not sure of something, liars will give a modified shrug when they are unsure of themselves. The liar's shrug is abnormal in that it is abridged and customized because the person manifesting it is not fully committed to what is being expressed. If only one shoulder comes up, or if the shoulders rise nearly to the ears and the person's head seems to disappear, it is a sign of high discomfort and sometimes seen in an individual preparing to answer a question deceptively.

CONCLUDING REMARKS

As I stated at the beginning of the chapter, the research over the last twenty years is unequivocal. There are no nonverbal behaviors that, in and of themselves, are clearly indicative of deception (Ekman, 1991, 98; Ford, 1996, 217). As my friend and researcher Dr. Mark G. Frank repeatedly has told me, "Joe, unfortunately, there is no 'Pinocchio effect,' when it comes to deception" (Frank, 2006). With that I must humbly concur. Therefore, in order to sort fact from fiction, our only realistic recourse is to rely on those behaviors indicative of comfort/discomfort, synchrony, and emphasis to guide us. They are a guide or paradigm, and that is all.

A person who is not comfortable, not emphasizing, and whose communication is out of synchrony is, at best, communicating poorly or, at worst, being deceptive. Discomfort may originate from many sources, including antipathy between those involved in the discussion, the setting in which the conversation is held, or nervousness during an interview process. It can also, obviously, be a result of culpability, guilty knowledge, having to hide information, or plain lying. The possibilities are many, but now that you know how better to question others, recognize their signs of discomfort, and the importance of putting their behaviors into context, at least you have a starting point. Only further inquiry, observation, and corroboration can assure us of veracity. There is no way we can prevent people from lying to us, but at least we can be on guard when they attempt to deceive us.

Last, be careful not to label someone a liar with limited information or based on one observation. Many good relationships have been ruined this way. Remember, when it comes to detecting deception, even the best experts, including myself, are only a blink away from chance, and have a fifty-fifty probability of being right or wrong. Plainly put, that's just not good enough!

NINE

Some Final Thoughts

A friend recently told me a story that speaks to the theme of this book and, incidentally, can save you significant hassles if you're ever trying to find an address in Coral Gables, Florida. This friend was driving her daughter to a photo shoot in Coral Gables, several hours from their home in Tampa. Because she had never been to Coral Gables before, she checked a map to determine the best route to follow. All went well until she arrived in town and started looking for street signs. There were none. She drove for twenty minutes through unmarked intersections, no signs in sight. Finally, in desperation, she stopped at a gas station and asked how anyone knew which street was which. The proprietor wasn't surprised by her question. "You're not the first to ask," he nodded sympathetically. "When you reach the intersection, you need to look down, not up. The street signs are six-inch weathered stone blocks with painted names and they are placed on the ground just off the pavement." My friend heeded his advice and within minutes located her destination. "Obviously," she noted, "I was looking for street signs six feet or more above the ground, not six inches off the ground. . . . What was most incredible," she added, "was once I knew what to look for and where to look, the signs were obvious and unmistakable. I had no trouble finding my way."

This book is about signs, too. When it comes to human behavior, there are basically two kinds of signs, verbal and nonverbal. All of us have been taught to look for and identify the verbal signs. By analogy, those are the ones that are located on poles, clearly visible as we drive down the streets of a strange city. Then there are the nonverbal signs, the ones that have always been there but that many of us have not learned to spot because we haven't been trained to look for and identify signs located at ground level. What's interesting is that once we learn to attend to and read nonverbal signs, our reactions will mirror that of my friend. "Once I knew what to look for and where to look, the signs were obvious and unmistakable. I had no trouble finding my way."

It is my hope that through an understanding of nonverbal behavior, you will achieve a deeper, more meaningful view of the world around you—able to hear and see the two languages, spoken and silent, that combine to present the full, rich tapestry of human experience in all of its delightful complexity. This is a goal well worth pursuing, and one that with effort I know you can achieve. You now possess something powerful. You possess knowledge that will enrich your interpersonal relationships for the rest of your life. Enjoy knowing what every *body* is saying, for to that end I have dedicated myself and this book.

Joe Navarro
Tampa, Florida
USA

BIBLIOGRAPHY

American Psychiatric Association. (2000). *Diagnostic and statistical manual of mental disorders* (4th ed.). Text rev. Washington, DC: American Psychiatric Association.

Axtell, R. E. (1991). *Gestures: The do's and taboos of body language around the world.* New York: John Wiley & Sons, Inc.

Burgoon, J. K., Buller, D. B., & Woodall, W. G. (1994). *Nonverbal communication: The unspoken dialogue.* Columbus, OH: Greyden Press.

Cialdini, R. B. (1993). *Influence: The psychology of persuasion.* New York: William Morrow and Company, Inc.

Collett, P. (2003). *The book of tells: From the bedroom to the boardroom—how to read other people.* Ontario: HarperCollins Ltd.

Cumming, A. Polygraph use by the Department of Energy: Issues for Congress (February 14, 2007): www.fas.org/sgp/crs/intel/RL31988.pdf.

Darwin, C. (1872). *The expression of emotion in man and animals.* New York: Appleton-Century Crofts.

de Becker, G. (1997). *The gift of fear.* New York: Dell Publishing.

DePaulo, B. M., Stone, J. I., & Lassiter, G. D. (1985). Deceiving and detecting deceit. In B. R. Schlenker (Ed.), *The self and social life.* New York: McGraw-Hill.

Diaz, B. (1988). *The conquest of new Spain*. New York: Penguin Books.

Dimitrius, J., & Mazzarella, M. (2002). *Put your best foot forward: Make a great impression by taking control of how others see you*. New York: Fireside.

———— (1998). *Reading people*. New York: Ballantine Books.

Ekman, P. (2003). *Emotions revealed: Recognizing faces and feelings to improve communication and emotional life*. New York: Times Books.

———— (1991). *Telling lies: Clues to deceit in the marketplace, politics, and marriage*. New York: W. W. Norton & Co.

Ekman, P., & O'Sullivan, M. (1991). Who can catch a liar? *American Psychologist* 46, 913–920.

Ford, C. V. (1996). *Lies! lies!! lies!!! The psychology of deceit*. Washington, DC: American Psychiatric Press, Inc.

Frank, M. G., et al. (2006). Investigative interviewing and the detection of deception. In Tom Williamson (Ed.), *Investigative interviewing: Rights, research, regulation*. Devon, UK: Willian Publishing.

Givens, D. B. (2005). *Love signals: A practical guide to the body language of courtship*. New York: St. Martin's Press.

———— (1998–2007). *The nonverbal dictionary of gestures, signs & body language cues*. Retrieved 11/18/07 from Spokane Center for Nonverbal Studies Web site: http://members.aol.com/nonverbal2/diction1.htm.

Goleman, D. (1995). *Emotional intelligence*. New York: Bantam Books.

Gregory, D. (1999). Personal conversation with Joe Navarro, FBI HQ, Washington, DC.

Grossman, D. (1996). *On killing: The psychological cost of learning to kill in war and society*. New York: Back Bay Books.

Hall, E. T. (1969). *The hidden dimension*. Garden City, NY: Anchor.

Hess, E. H. (1975a). *The tell-tale eye: How your eyes reveal hidden thoughts and emotions*. New York: Van Nostrand Reinhold.

———— (1975b). The role of pupil size in communication. *Scientific American* 233, 110–119.

Johnson, R. R. (2007). Race and police reliance on suspicious non-verbal cues. *Policing: An International Journal of Police Strategies & Management* 20 (2), 277–290.

Kassin, S. M. (2006). A critical appraisal of modern police interrogations. In Tom Williamson (Ed.), *Investigative interviewing: Rights, research, regulation*. Devon, UK: Willian Publishing.

———— (2004). True or false: "I'd know a false confession if I saw one." In Pär Anders Granhag & Leif A. Strömwall (Eds.), *The detection of deception in forensic contexts*. Cambridge, UK: Cambridge University Press.

Knapp, M. L., & Hall, J. A. (2002). *Nonverbal communication in human interaction*, (5th Ed.). New York: Harcourt Brace Jovanovich.

Leakey, R. E., & Lewin, R. (1977). *Origins: The emergence and evolution of our species and its possible future*. New York: E. P. Dutton.

LeDoux, J. (1996). *The emotional brain: The mysterious underpinnings of emotional life*. New York: Touchstone.

Lieberman, D. J. (1998). *Never be lied to again*. New York: St. Martin's Press.

Manchester, W. (1978). *American Caesar: Douglas MacArthur 1880–1964*. Boston: Little, Brown, & Company.

Morris, D. (1985). *Body watching*. New York: Crown Publishers.

Murray, E. (2007). Interviewed by Joe Navarro, August 18, Ontario, Canada.

Myers, D. G. (1993). *Exploring psychology* (2nd ed). New York: Worth Publishers.

Navarro, J. (2007). *Psychologie de la communication non verbale*. In M. St-Yues & M. Tanguay (Eds.), *Psychologie de l'enquête criminelle: La recherche de la vérité*. Cowansville, Québec: Les Éditions Yvon Blais: 141–163.

———— (2006). *Read 'em and reap: A career FBI agent's guide to decoding poker tells*. New York: HarperCollins.

———— (2003). A four-domain model of detecting deception. *FBI Law Enforcement Bulletin* (June), 19–24.

Navarro, J., & Schafer, J. R. (2003). Universal principles of criminal behavior: A tool for analyzing criminal intent. *FBI Law Enforcement Bulletin* (January), 22–24.

———— (2001). Detecting deception. *FBI Law Enforcement Bulletin* (July), 9–13.

Nolte, J. (1999). *The human brain: An introduction to its functional anatomy*. St. Louis, MO: Mosby.

Ost, J. (2006). Recovered memories. In Tom Williamson (Ed.), *Investigative interviewing: Rights, research, regulation*. Devon, UK: Willian Publishing.

Panksepp, J. (1998). *Affective neuroscience: The foundations of human and animal emotions*. New York: Oxford University Press, Inc.

Prkachin, K. M., & Craig, K. D. (1995). Expressing pain: The communication and interpretation of facial pain signals. *Journal of Nonverbal Behavior* 9 (4), Winter, 181–205.

Ratey, J. J. (2001). *A user's guide to the brain: Perception, attention, and the four theaters of the brain*. New York: Pantheon Books.

Schafer, J. R., & Navarro, J. (2004). *Advanced interviewing techniques*. Springfield, IL: Charles C. Thomas Publisher.

Simons, D. J., & Chabris, C. F. (1999). Gorillas in our midst: Sustained inattentional blindness for dynamic events. *Perception 28*, 1059–1074.

St-Yves, M., & Tanguay, M. (Eds.) (2007). *Psychologie de l'enquête criminelle: La recherche de la vérité*. Cowansville, Québec: Les Éditions Yvon Blais.

Vrij, A. (2003). *Detecting lies and deceit: The psychology of lying and the implications for professional practice*. Chichester, UK: John Wiley & Sons, Ltd.

INDEX

(page numbers in *italics* refer to illustrations)

ALSO BY JOE NAVARRO

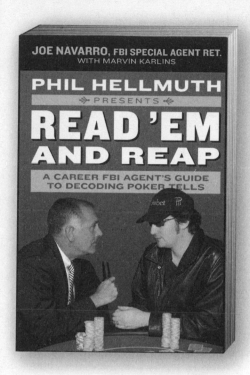

PHIL HELLMUTH PRESENTS READ 'EM AND REAP

A CAREER FBI AGENT'S GUIDE TO DECODING POKER TELLS

ISBN 978-0-06-119859-5
(paperback)

Every great player knows that success in poker is part luck, part math, and part subterfuge. While the math of poker has been refined over the past 20 years, the ability to read other players and keep your own "tells" in check has mostly been learned by trial and error.

But now, Joe Navarro, a former FBI counterintelligence officer specializing in nonverbal communication and behavior analysis—or, to put it simply, a man who can tell when someone's lying—offers foolproof techniques, illustrated with amazing examples from poker pro Phil Hellmuth, that will help you decode and interpret your opponents' body language and other silent tip-offs while concealing your own. You'll become a human lie detector, ready to call every bluff—and the most feared player in the room.

COLLINS LIVING
An Imprint of HarperCollins Publishers
www.harpercollins.com